TREES
IN
URBAN HABITAT

HARDIAL SINGH JOHL

SARBJIT SINGH BAHGA

PHOTOGRAPHY
SANYAM BAHGA
BALJIT SINGH

Trees in Urban Habitat

This book is dedicated to my daughter Perneet
who incited me into writing it.

Hardial Singh Johl

Contents

Preface

The main focus of this book is to present an ideal use of trees in urban living with the goal of significantly improving the quality of life for people living and working in urban areas. To achieve this objective we conducted a thorough study of New Delhi's architecturally designed tree plantation plans done by Sir Edwin Lutyens and those done by Le Corbusier for Chandigarh. Both of them are world famous architects, planners and designers. Growing trees is the cheapest and one of the most effective methods for improving the physical environment. Trees are the most exquisite natural material for urban design. Most of our urban habitats have high densities of population, are treeless, bare and are facing alarming levels of pollution. It is necessary to take up a tree plantation programme at the national level. Trees purify dirty air, reduce dust, noise and create a healthy, livable environment.

This book highlights the fundamental requirements of carrying out plantation in a planned manner around roads, buildings, open spaces and parks etc. All over India, planned and designed urban growth is taking place at rapid pace and on a large scale. People desire attractive and functional trees on roads, in play areas, in work places and it can be created! That is what this book does, presents the concept of developing the entire city as a park.

Human artistry can improve by shaping the materials of the city including trees to create a better urban habitat. One can plan and grow trees not as decoration but as living building materials to create and reinforce urban spaces. This is achieved by planting trees as groups in the form of rows, groves and numerous architectural settings in accordance with the intrinsic nature and evolutionary requirements, not as scattered individual specimens.

At present carefully designed road sections and proper places for growing trees and installation of electric power lines are not being adopted even in the planned cities. This aspect is indispensable and has been explained in great detail in this book. The right kind of walkways along roads for pedestrian movement too is absolutely needed. This too has been dealt in this text.

This book also contains some of important trees suitable for planting around city roads, buildings, open spaces and parks. The salient features of these trees are described and demonstrated with photographs.

Our hope is that the approach of tree plantation as described in this book gets adopted in urban areas. That will produce wonderful results and will serve as a model for all present and future generations.

This study will be beneficial to town planners, architects, landscape architects, horticulturists, engineers and all other professionals and administrators engaged in the task of planning cities and plantations in urban areas.

Applicability of this book in other countries of the world

The work on trees in this book pertains mostly to New Delhi designed by Lutyens about a century ago and Chandigarh planned by Le Corbusier, the world famous architect which came in being six decades ago. Both these cities are located in the sub tropical regions of India which obtain extremes of climate in summer and winter months. The summers are very hot and winters are very cold. The major rainfall occurs mainly in monsoon season that is, July - August, and for the remaining year the weather remains dry with occasional showers. The trees appropriate for growing around roads, open spaces, parks and buildings as described in this book are suitable for the climatic conditions obtained in both these cities. These trees however, would perform much better in tropical parts of the country where rainfall is much more during the year and summer and winter seasons are milder with little variations in temperature and are congenial for growth of the trees.

Some of the other countries of the world that have tropical and subtropical climate will also be suitable for growing many kinds of trees discussed in the book. The species in other countries may be different but the fundamental requirements for tree plantation in the urban habitat are applicable anywhere and everywhere in the world, wherever tree culture is done. Some of these countries where similar kinds of trees are grown are:

Burma(Myanmar), **Thailand**, **Sri Lanka**, **Vietnam**, **Bangladesh**, **Malaysia**, **Pakistan**, **Java**, **Philippines**, **Laos**, **Indonesia**, **Sumatra**, **Singapore**, **Southern China**, **Taiwan**, **Cambodia**, **Tropical Australia** and **Northern Australia**, **Tropical Africa**, **Madagascar**, **Tropical South America** consisting of **Brazil**, **Argentina**, **Colombia**, **Peru**, **Bolivia**, and **Chile** etc. Tropical areas in **Mexico** as well as south-east and central regions of **United States of America** also obtain suitable climatic conditions for growth of similar kind of species.

Even in countries where tree culture is done, the fundamental requirements for planting of trees around the roads, open spaces, parks and buildings remain the same and are applicable as narrated in this book.

Acknowledgements

I dedicate this book to my daughter, Perneet who inspired me to write this book and accomplish my objective of giving back to the community of urban planners and designers. She encouraged me to share my knowledge and experience that I have gathered from my decades contributing to landscaping. I have compiled my knowledge in this book for use to those engaged in the task of urban planning and improving the physical environment of the human beings living in cities.

I am particularly grateful to my sons, Ajai Johl and Amandeep Johl for their contributions in enthusing me with innovative thoughts and helping improve the quality of text. Ricki too helped me in many ways for which I express my gratitude to her.

I am highly indebted to Sarbjit Bahga, an eminent architect, for his commitment and support throughout this project. He has written many books of international fame and is an expert in the art of designing and arranging presentation of entire manuscript in an ideal manner. I owe the success of this project entirely to him. I am also grateful to his family– wife Gurdeep Kaur and sons Arshdeep and Supreet– for their support as they came along this journey with me. His brother, Surinder Bahga also offered valuable suggestions and cooperation in compiling this book.

My special thanks to Sanyam Bahga and Baljit Singh both exceptional photographers. My special thanks to them in making the script come alive with their photography. I am grateful for the editing work done by Amit Roy, a well-known journalist with exquisite work for many outstanding newspapers of India like "Hindustan Times". I am very appreciative of Deeksha Sachdeva and Shanni Kumar who are amazing experts in design. They helped in the preparation of elaborate tree plantation plans for buildings, parks as well as sketches of road sections.

My deepest sense of gratitude to my wife, Gurbrinder, for her constant support, encourage-ment and positive energy. She has been patient through the endless hours of research and effort that she remained deprived of my companionship.

Hardial Singh Johl

About Authors

Hardial Singh Johl

Hardial Singh Johl (b 1933) is an experienced and renowned landscapist. He got his Masters degree from Punjab Agriculture University, Ludhiana (formerly Punjab College of Agriculture) in 1955. He started his career as the landscape designer at the famous Mughal gardens of Pinjore. He worked in Chandigarh for over two decades where he revitalized the landscape plans of the city. During his tenure as head of Chandigarh's landscaping wing he designed and developed the entire city, including roads, avenues, several parks and gardens. The world famous Rose Garden is a product of his expertise and design. He then worked for the Punjab government as head of the Landscape Circle. He also served as landscape Advisor to Punjab Urban Development Authority and developed the urban estates of Mohali, Ludhiana, Jalandhar, Patiala and Bathinda. His master projects include the Punjabi University campus in Patiala, Silver City in Zirakhpur, the Coach factory at Kapurthala and the historical city of Anandpur Sahib. His contribution to landscape and landscape design includes over 300 articles in the daily newspaper, The Tribune. He has received recognition from several leading administrators and professionals in this field.

Sarbjit Singh Bahga

Sarbjit Singh Bahga (b1957) is a Chandigarh based architect, urbanist, author and photo-artist. He graduated in architecture from Panjab University, Chandigarh in 1979 and was conferred with Doctorate in Architectural Science (D.A.S.) in 2000. He works in the Department of Architecture, Punjab and has 33 years of practical experience in designing and supervision of various types of buildings, complexes and large campuses. He is presently working on deputation as Senior Architect in the Punjab Mandi Board, Chandigarh. His completed works include an eclectic and impressive range of medical, educational, administrative, commercial, recreational and residential buildings. His buildings are interesting and responsive to function, climate and materials. He is a staunch modernist and an ardent, yet not blind, admirer of Le Corbusier, Pierre Jeanneret and Louis Kahn. Sarbjit is  also a keen researcher, a prolific architectural writer, and a Fellow of United Writers' Association of India. He has six books to his credit. His books, Modern Architecture in India: Post-Independence Perspective (1993), New Indian Homes: An Architectural Renaissance (1996) and Le Corbusier & Pierre Jeanneret: Footprints on the Sands of Indian Architecture are considered as landmarks in the history of contemporary architecture of India. Apart from this, he is a keen photo-artist especially in the field of architectural photography and has won many awards in this field. Bahga takes special interest in the overall development of profession of architecture and improvement of built-environment. He is an active member of many professional associations including the Indian Institute of Architects. His contribution to architecture has been largely recognized and his buildings/articles have been widely published in many architectural journals and books.

1
IMPORTANCE OF TREES IN URBAN PLANNING

1.1 Tees January Marg, New Delhi: Designed by Edwin Lutyens, a British architect, 100 years ago, large structural Neem trees (Azadirachta indica) on this road have created extensive green cover between buildings and roads, enhancing the beauty of the street and buildings, and all spaces around the road.

WORSHIPPING of trees dates backs to hundreds of years in our traditionally rich country. Trees are also an essential component of a habitat. Britishers deserve credit for making good use of this natural resource. They played an important role in developing beautiful parks and gardens not only in dak bungalows and New Delhi roads but also in prosaic places like district courts. However, after independence, the focus shifted to developing infrastructure and no attention was paid to greening and tree plantation with the exception of cities like Chandigarh.

Every city needs beautiful environs, which not only adds aesthetic value to the city but also provides a green and healthy environment for its residents. All living beings need a healthy environment for sustenance and if they are kept away from nature, they start to perish. Trees are the vital and exquisite elements that add life and soul to a city that is otherwise made up of brick and mortar. Apart from contributing to the basic requirements of humans, trees help in sprucing up cities in many ways:

- They enhance the beauty of streets, buildings, parks and all spaces in a

1.2 Tuglak Road, New Delhi: Continuous and repetitive use of a single kind of Jamboa tree (Eugenia operculata) brought about cohesiveness and enhanced the entire landscape. Its plantation on road verge has separated vehicular and pedestrian passage. Designed by Edwin Lutyens - a British architect and planner.

city including work, shopping and recreational spaces.

- They bind the entire city design components. Continuous and repetitive use of trees brings about a cohesiveness that enhances the entire landscape. On the contrary, spaces that are treeless look bare, monotonous and drab.

- They help make living spaces; green walls, ceilings and outdoor rooms creating a spectacular effect. Large structured trees, with big branches, thick foliage provide a green cover over the structural elements of a city.

- Above all, they help create the macro and micro climate of cities. They provide shelter from sweltering heat and glare of summer, sleet and blast of winters, help in reducing global warming, air pollution, dirt in the air and noise, also ensuring the health efficiency and productivity of human beings.

Trees add greenery around us but it's important they are arranged according to fundamental design concepts i.e. spacing, density, size, form. Collective use of species

1.3 Jan Path Road, New Delhi: Large structured Arjan trees (Terminalia arjuna) with big branches, thick foliage have developed green walls, ceilings and outdoor rooms creating a spectacular effect. Designed by Edwin Lutyens - a British Architect and Planner.

according to scale and required dimensions can meet all functional requirements and also add beauty. Instead of scattering trees, using them collectively in groves, rows, and symmetrical units can create balance and harmony.

Cities that are well planned need to be well planted as well for them to serve as the nucleus of culture in urban habitats. Such cities can provide congenial living conditions that are traditionally thought to be found in rural pastoral areas.

There is no denying in the fact that most of our urban habitat is drab and denuded of vegetation. The degradation of

our environment in big cities has attained alarming proportions for lack of effective green cover. Almost all our cities with high density of population are treeless, bare and dull and with coming up of new buildings and widening of roads, the tree cover is fast depleting. Cities, small towns and villages are facing dense populations and the entire countryside which was once our untouched serene heritage is fast disappearing. During the last about six decades, haphazard urbanization and industrial growth has brought about tremendous changes around us.

1.4 Krishna Menon Marg, New Delhi: Ficus amplissima has created an attractive evergreen roof of big arching branches and beautiful foliage - enhancing the beauty of the street. Designed by Edwin Lutyens - a British architect and planner.

While urbanization is important and is a continuous process, unprecedented growth is taking place both in the public and private sectors. This is a challenge for planners who have to incorporate this growth into their plans. It is creditable that in recent times urban development authorities have taken over management of urban areas in our country. Their exemplary work is evident in good infrastructure that we are so familiar with - good buildings and roads, electric lines, good public health facilities, planned recreational sites, global connectivity through airports and rail networks etc.

Unfortunately our town planning laws do not provide for tree plantation as an essential part of a city plan. They are only involved with providing good infrastructure i.e. buildings, roads, electricity and good public health. Landscaping of road berms through small floral plantations is done but tree plantation has never been considered important. Tree plantation today is the need of the hour and must be a mandatory part of any city plan.

1.5 Neem tree (Azadirachta indica) avenue in Chandigarh: Large structured unique Neem tree on V5 road in Chandigarh has created distinctive personality. Repeated use of single kind of tree has created healthy tall green walls. Its branches have intermingled and developed a continuous net work which looks splendid.

The Opportunity at Hand

Having a good green cover has its benefits which we have realized in the recent past. This offers an opportunity to step up and act now so that our cities do not lose their sheen. We must think about the community as a whole and not just a select few because having green surroundings are for betterment of all.

People need planned cities, which are convenient, comfortable and a pleasure to live in and work. Who doesn't love leafy lanes and lovely trees and colourful flowers? Then why not ensure that we all get them? It is not just a need of the present generation but the right of the future generations too.

Lutyen's, New Delhi and Corbusier's Chandigarh are the only two cities in India where tree plantation has got high priority and has been done in a planned manner. There has been intensive study on tree plantation work done in both these cities.

It has been found that as far as Lutyen's, New Delhi is concerned, masterful work was undertaken in almost every aspect. High priority was given to the structure of the tree and indigenous species which can develop tall strong trunks and spreading crowns were used. Also pure avenues of single kind of trees were planted close to the road curb separating the vehicular and pedestrian traffic.

Arrangement of trees was also done in a

1.6 Kigelia pinnata avenue in Chandigarh: Large structured Kigelia tree with big branches has developed green walls, provided complete ceiling on the entire wide road. Single kind of tree has brought about complete homogeneity of structure, texture and foliage creating wonderful effect.

well planned manner that gives an attractive look. Flowering trees were planted in parks, open spaces and around public buildings which is the right place for such kinds of trees.

Chandigarh city came into being almost four decades after New Delhi. It happens to be perfect example of a city where different varieties of plants and trees have been planted from all over the world. The tree plantation here has played an important role in improving the quality of life in the city. **Corbusier gave high priority to tree plantation due to which significant results have been produced and substantial achievements have been made in this direction, but an ideal state of tree plantation has not been achieved**.

Chandigarh is a perfect example where several outstanding varieties of trees are planted on city roads. These include trees that are structurally big, have tall strong trunks and spreading crowns. Most of the important roads have been planted with single kind of tree species in a well-planned manner. The trees in this city have spruced up the streets, buildings and all spaces around roads. Repeated use of trees has brought about cohesiveness due to homogeneity of structure, texture and pattern, and has greatly improved the entire landscape of the city. Trees have developed lovely green walls, ceilings, created outdoor rooms with their big branches, attractive foliage and have provided green covers around the architecturally well-planned

1.7 Jan Marg Chandigarh: This road has been most extensively planted with mostly Chukrasia tree (Chukrasia tabularis) which gives a comforting effect to those using the road. Massive plantation of almost single kind of tree has brought about cohesiveness and has enhanced the landscape.

buildings of the city. Pictorially illustrated are some of the best avenues that show the wonderful work done in this city.

This book focuses on the use of trees in a designed manner. It contains an in-depth study carried out regarding tree plantation work done in New Delhi and Chandigarh, the only two cities in our country where lot of importance and priority has been given to tree plantation.

Photographs and illustrations support the fundamental concepts that are emphasized in this book. A detailed study and description of some important avenues and roadside plantations in Chandigarh, as well as open spaces, parks and buildings etc. is included.

The book also contains fundamental requirements pertaining to structure of trees, texture, shape and form, colour, arrangement, spacing, diversity and scale etc. which are the most important considerations for obtaining excellent planting design in urban areas.

Illustrations and discussions of these topics highlight "lessons learnt" and provide an opportunity for improved future planning and development of cities. Brief descriptions of some very outstanding trees that are suitable for our towns for various locations such as city roads, streets, open spaces, parks, public and private buildings have been given along with photographs. Included with all this are practical methods to raise trees in cities to obtain outstanding results in this task.

1.8 Himalaya Marg, Chandigarh: This road has been decorated with Kusum tree (Schleichera oleosa) which has got colourful foliage and gives mass effect of bright red and yellow colours in different seasons. The avenue has developed green walls, ceilings and outdoor rooms creating a spectacular effect.

1.9 Udyog Marg, Chandigarh: A beautiful, green and fascinating tree plantation with Swietenia macrophylla tree has brought about change in the quality of life in the city. Its continuous and repetitive use has brought about cohesiveness and enhanced the beauty of the city's landscape.

2

ABOUT LUTYENS NEW DELHI

THE Indian capital, New Delhi, a city which came into being 100 years ago is an exemplary work of urban planning.Sir Edwin Landseer Lutyens conceptualized the city's Master Plan which broadly consists of the Presidential Estate, Janpath and India Gate in the Central Vista with Connaught Place on the one side and Lodhi Road on the other.

Sir Lutyens also created the the landscape design of this part of the city. He collaborated with William Robertson Mustow, a gardener and Walter George, a town planner in planning, selecting, planting and maintaining this stretch of the city.

Lutyens worked with a very short list of trees that were known to possibly grow in New Delhi. This list was prepared by Griessen of the Horticulture Department of New Delhi. It consisted primarily of indigenous species of trees such as Neem (Azadirachta indica), Arjan (Terminalia arjuna), Jamboa (Engenia operculata), Jadi (Ficus amplissima), Imli (Tamarindus indica), Bahera (Terminalia bellirica), Tree of heaven (Ailanthus excelsa) etc. Lutyens used these trees on almost all the roads he planned and planted.

2.1 Neem tree (Azadirachta indica), planted on Tees January Marg. Single kind of evergreen Neem tree created glorious collective impact due to homogeneity of structure, texture and pattern. This tree has also been extensively used on Prithviraj road , Aurangzeb road, Ashok road, Safdarjang road and Lodhi Road .

2.2 Arjan tree (Terminalia arjuna) planted on Janpath. Arjan tree planted close to the verge has separated vehicular traffic and pedestrian movement and looks fantastic. Arjan has also been planted on Teen Murti and Mother Teresa Marg.

2.3 Jamboa (Engenia operculata) planted on Motilal Nehru Marg, New Delhi. Jamboa tree is structurally big and evergreen. Its high trunk, well formed crowns provides complete cover with spreading and dropping branches and foliage -making the avenue functional and attractive. Plantation of Jamboa has been repeated on Tughlak road, Rajaji road as well as Tyagraj Marg.

Tree plantation in New Delhi is one of a kind! It is a an exemplary model of architectural, structural and aesthetic excellence. Some of the remarkable features that can be attributed to its artistry are:

- Use of structurally large trees with very tall, straight trunks that form excellent sprawling crowns.

- The use of indigenous species that are hardy, sturdy and durable that makes them easy to grow and maintain. They are able to withstand the extreme environmental pollution from toxic automobile exhausts that usually threaten delicate trees.

- Evergreen varieties of trees used which lends to year-round green effect and protection from severe weather conditions.

- The entire expanse of open space between the concrete buildings and roads covered, creating a soothing visual effect.

- Avenues planted with single kind of trees that offers a glorious collective impact. The consistency, homogeneity of structure, texture and pattern it creates has helped bind the entire city together.

- Trees planted in straight rows and geometric patterns help create a beautiful effect in a city the magnitude of Delhi.

- Planting trees close to the verges, has helped separate vehicular and pedestrian traffic.

In Addition

- All flowering species of trees that are structurally small, short-lived and difficult to grow and maintain have deliberately not been used for roadside plantation. Instead these have been exclusively planted in parks and various open spaces where they grow well and provide colour and beauty to the city.

2.4 Tree of heaven (Ailanthus excelsa) planted on Copernicus Marg, New Delhi. Tree of heaven is tall, stately and majestic. Being structurally large tree, it has lent distinct character to this road.

2.5 Jadi (Ficus amplissima) has been planted on Krishna Menon Marg, New Delhi. Jadi tree has developed evergreen cover on the entire wide space between concrete buildings and road. It creates a wonderful high roof of branches andproviding a soothing visual effect.

2.6 Imli (Tamarindus indica) planted on Akbar road. Imli tree decorates Akbar road with tall straight trunk, spreading crown, providing green cover on the entire road and pedestrian path separating vehicular and pedestrian traffic. Imli tree has also been planted on Tilak road, Pandit Pant Marg and a stretch of Mother Teresa Marg.

Looking back, there are a few things that could have been done differently resulting in a better outcome.

Limited varieties of trees were used and that too repeatedly on different avenues leading to monotony. At the time that Lutyens was designing and planning there were several other good varities, which could have been included in the list that he worked with. Tree plantation plan of Lutyens' New Delhi roads would have made a significant mark if the Horticulture Department of New Delhi had provided him the knowhow of other outstanding species of trees for plantation on New Delhi roads. Names and photographs of some of these are given below:

2.8 Chukrasia tabularis (Modern Neem)

2.7 Terminalia myriocarpa (Hollock)

2.9 Ficus microcarpa (Indian Laurel Tree)

2.10 Schleichera oleosa (Kusum)

2.11 Bischofia javanica (Bishopwood)

2.12 Swietenia macrophylla (Mahagony)

All these varieties are indigenous, structurally large trees having excellent trunks and crowns. They are evergreen, sturdy, hardy, durable, neat, and do not litter. They are extremely functional trees and can withstand environmental pollution. They are also magnificent trees, that meet all the aesthetic requirements, require minimum care and are ideally suited to the agro-climatic conditions in New Delhi. If these were used, the entire tree plantation plan of the national capital would have become an ideal model for the entire country.

Secondly, the trees could have been planted closer to each other. The trees on Delhi roads as we see them today would not have taken over 50 years to create the desired effect, had they been planted at smaller distances from each other. The tall trunks and large rounded crowns would have had the desired impact much sooner than they actually did. While the challenge with growing the trees too close to each other is that the tree develops a denser lower branched crown not attaining the real height of the tree for a much longer period than it should, they can be planted at a reasonable distance apart where they do not run into that problem but at the same time do not take too long to create the desired effect.

The photographs (2.13, 2.14 and 2.15) in this chapter speak the story detailed in this chapter. Large, long trunked trees have attained the height of more than 20 feet producing broad views of extensive areas of the city that are clearly visible in vast continuous avenues. At the same time the top arches of the trees give a spectacular visual appearance of a dense canopy extending over the horizon. The trees define the magnificence of the city !

2.13 Neem tree (Azadirachta indica) planted on Aurangzeb road at a very wide spacing of 40-50 feet (centre to centre).

2.14 Neem tree (Azadirachta indica) planted on Tees January Marg. It took more than 50 years to obtain the desired effect because the trees were planted at a spacing of 40-50 feet. Tall trunks and extensive crowns would have filled up the entire spaces in a very short period if these were closely planted.

2.15 Arjan tree (Terminalia arjuna) planted on Janpath at a very wide spacing of 40-50 feet (centre to centre).

3

LE CORBUSIER'S CHANDIGARH

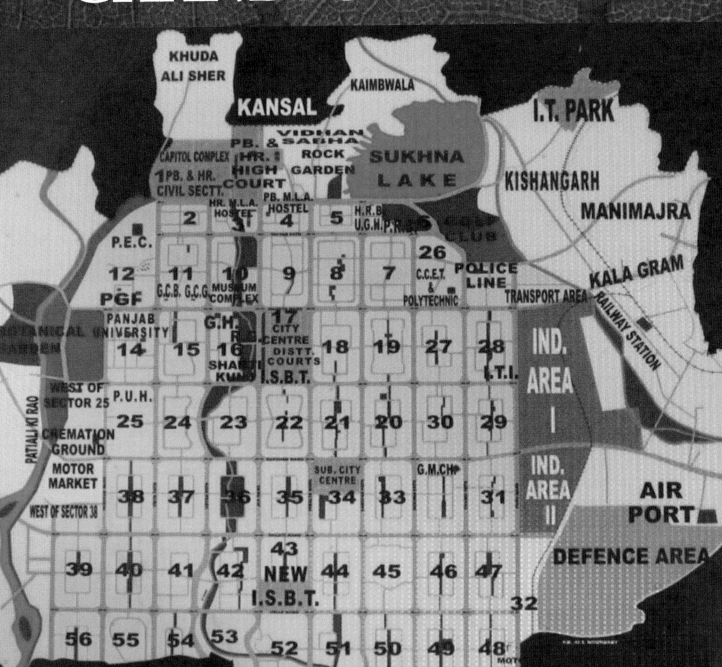

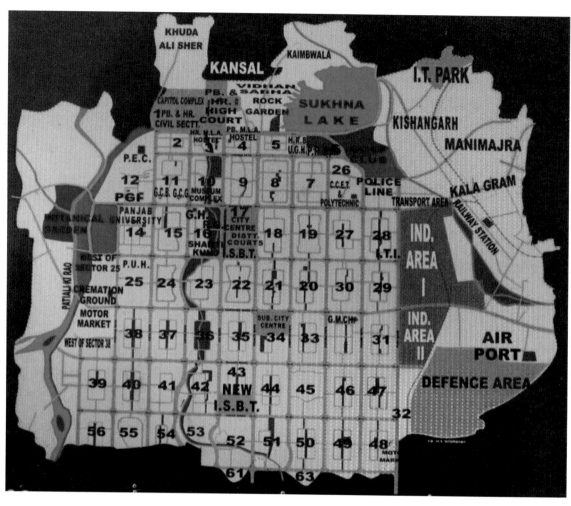

3.1 Master Plan of Chandigarh designed by Monsieur Le Corbusier.

CHANDIGARH, the modern city of independent India was founded in the year 1953. It was meant to be a symbol of the progress the nation had made and at the same time a model for the future urban life in India.

Charles-Edouard Jeanneret, better known as Le Corbusier was a world famous architect and planner. Le Corbusier, with architects Pierre Jeanneret, Maxwell Fry and Jane Drew, were instrumental in making the master plan of Chandigarh. They brought vast global experience and knowledge to cater to the needs of the region to create this beautiful city. **Le-Corbusier gave great importance to verger of the city. According to him Sun, Space and Verger are the most essential natural requirements of all the living beings and without these they tend to perish.**

Chandigarh has come to be internationally renowned as the "City Beautiful" because of its intelligent planning, architecture and landscaping. It is one of the most thoughtfully planned cities in India. While the architectural beauty is exceptional what makes the city truly striking is the fine accentuation of the structures with trees and greenery. The landscape design of Chandigarh has offered it to attain the status of a garden city.

3.2 Monsieur Le Corbusier (1887-1965)

3.3 Dr. M.S. Randhawa, Administrator of Chandigarh. Enriched city with lovely flora from all over the world.

The infrastructure of plant life created here is in itself a very big achievement. The city roads and streets have been planted aesthetically and several gardens have been manicured. Dr. M.S. Randhawa, the first Administrator of the city was a plant lover and played a key role in beautifying the city. He encouraged the collection of decorative plants and trees from all over the world. The result was that the city got enriched with an extensive collection of all kinds of beautiful fauna from different parts of India as well as other parts of the world.

Le Corbusier and Dr Randhawa constituted a landscape committee of experts in Chandigarh. The committee put together a comprehensive list of plants and trees with details on their shapes, colours and textures. The list comprised of beautiful, ornamental, flowering and foliage trees. These trees were the foundation of tree planting in Chandigarh. It is because of emphasis on shape and colour that defined landscaping in Chandigarh.

Concepts of tree plantation applied in Chandigarh

In Chandigarh, typically crown shape and seasonal colour were the important and major determinants in selecting a tree type for city road plantation. Chart showing classification of trees according to shape of crown and color of flower has been displayed on the following page. The emphasis on roadside tree plantation was cosmetic beautification. Flowering trees were meant to be used as embellishments to architectural structures of the city. As a result the flowering trees which do not inherently grow large enough were extensively used to decorate exterior spaces of the city, not realizing that being small in size they never create the much needed high canopies and arching roof of branches and foliage. Thus, their use in public spaces remains decorative yet inappropriate.

CLASSIFICATION OF TREES ACCORDING TO SHAPE OF CROWN AND COLOUR OF FLOWERS

SHAPE OF TREES	COLOUR OF FLOWERS						
	Green	Light yellow	Yellow	Red	Mauve	Purple	Pink
	*Chukrasia tabularis *Swietenia macrophylla *Bischofia javanica *Schleichera oleosa *Azadirachta indica *Kigelia pinnata *Madhuca latifolia *Cinnamomum camphora *Artocarpus lacucha	*Pterospermum acerifolium *Crataeva religiosa *Albizia procera *Dillenia indica	*Cassia fistula *Schleichera oleosa *Anthocephalus cadamba *Cassia spectabilis	* Schleichera oleosa *Spathodea campanulata *Erythrina indica *Delonix regia *Saraca indica *Butea Monosperma *Koelreuteria elegans	*Jacaranda mimosifolia	*Kigelia pinnata *Millettia ovalifolia *Lagerstroemia thorellii *Lagerstroemia flos reginae	*Cassia javanica *Cassia nodosa *Cassia renigera *Bauhinia variegate *Lagerstroemia rosea
	*Ficus microcarpa *Ficus infectoria *Ficus religiosa *Ficus amplissima *Eugenia operculata *Tamarindus indica * Haplophragma adenophyllum	*Plumeria acutifolia *Plumeria alba	*Thespesia populnea *Peltophorum ferrugineum	*Delonix regia *Plumeria rubra *Diospyros embryopteris		*Pongamia glabra	*Enterolobium saman
	*Hardwickia binata *Terminalia arjuna *Terminalia bellerica *Terminalia myriocarpa *Casuarina equisetifolia *Acrocarpus fraxinifolius *Alstonia scholaris * Azadirachta burmanica * Alianthus excelsa *Cedrela toona *Pinus longifolia *Agathis robusta	*Bauhinia acuminata *Terminalia myriocarpa *Michelia alba	*Grevillea robusta *Cassia siamea *Acacia auriculiformis *Tecomella undulata *Tecoma argentea	*Terminalia myriocarpa *Colvillea racemosa *Bombax malabaricum *Sapium sebiferum (foliage turns red)		*Tabebuia rosea	*Chorisia speciosa
	*Polyalthia longifolia *Sterculia alata *Sterculia foetida *Podocarpus gracilior *Taxodium mucranatum *Araucaria cookie	*Millingtonia hortensis					
	*Salix babylonica *Polyalthia longifolia variety pendula		*Callistemon having yellow foliage	*Callistemon lanceolatus	Callistemon having mauve foliage		

Chart showing classification of trees according to shape of crown and colour of flowers. This chart was one of the most essential element which constituted the problem of landscaping and tree plantation in Chandigarh. The entire tree plantation work around city roads, open spaces, parks and buildings was done keeping in view both of these considerations i.e., shape of crown and colour of flowers. Due to this reason perfection in the task could not be realised.

Furthermore, they obstruct the architectural views of the city buildings because of their low branched dense crowns. Flowering trees have short blooming periods, varying from two to four weeks in a year. The rest of the year they stand devoid of flowers and their structure and foliage does not add much beauty to the city roads.

They also are difficult to grow and maintain and are short-lived. As a result most of them have not survived for more than 2-3 decades especially around roads where they are exposed to vehicular pollution. The outcome of this has been that Chandigarh roads have developed gaps that have been filled by miscellaneous hardy species of trees. This has adversely affected the quality of landscape in Chandigarh and is contrary to a fundamental of tree plantation i.e. planting one kind of trees on a particular road to attain aesthetic beauty.

Apart from small structured flowering trees, the shape of the crown formed an important concept for tree plantation in Chandigarh. To maintain the shape of the crown and "open grown form" plantation was done at wide spaces. Spacing of trees is of immense aesthetic importance. Trees placed "too far apart" develop a dense, low branched crown. They do not form the required tall roof of foliage and branches. They also adversely affect the broad views of the city, cause obstruction in the movement of traffic, reduce light and take a long time, sometimes decades to fill up the spaces in-between. Thus, the "open grown form" of a tree is suitable for decorative use either as a separate piece of sculpture or as part of a group since they do not perform the primary function of creating and binding spaces.

3.5 Vidya Path - 100 feet wide road between Sector 2 and 11. Milletia ovalifolia flowering tree structurally very small, did not create much needed canopies. Also these trees never develop straight trunk and high branched crown to create a ceiling and green cover on the entire V3 road which is one of the most essential requirement.

3.6 Entire view of Vidya Path around Sector 2 and 11. Road looks bare without roof of tree branches and foliage. Doesnot meet scale requirement.

Trees should be planted "too close" together and not as scattered individuals. The practice of close plantation is also necessary in view of the intrinsic nature and evolutionary requirements of trees. Closely planted trees develop upright, high branched crowns, form excellent grooves, and fill up spaces in the shortest possible period to form avenues of trees that are very functional and aesthetically attractive.

3.7 Shopping street 44 feet wide in Sector 18. Cassia Siamea flowering tree inherently small, blocked view of shops and reduced street space. Grown for decorative purpose only. Many gaps have developed on this important V4 road which have been planted with numerous kinds of trees thus adversely affecting the quility of landscape. Moreover the entire road and parking area are without the green cover.

3.8 Circulation road (V5) 60 feet wide in Sector 7. Plantation of Acacia auriculiformis tree reduced the street space and blocked view of residential homes. It does not provide green cover on the streat.

3.9 Circulation road (V5) 60 feet wide in sector 16. Tecomella undulata - a small flowering tree grown for the purpose of embellishment only. The entire plantation on this road is haphazardly planted with various kinds of small structured flowering trees which are unsuitable and do not meet the required function.

3.10 Vidya Path between Panjab University and Sector 15. The entire road is without green ceiling which is one of the most essential reqiurements.

3.11 Circulation road Sector 16. Mixtures of Tecomella undulata and Bauhinia flowering trees have reduced the size of the street space - made it narrow. Also views of homes blocked. Trees being small structured do not provide green cover on the entire road.

Despite all these factors, Chandigarh proudly maintains the status of the Garden city and is considered the greenest city in India. This has been possible due to the large outstanding varieties of trees that are very suitable of road plantations. These have been extensively used on most roads as pure avenues of a single kind of species. They are structurally big, with excellent foliage, spreading crowns and have produced great results making Chandigarh an outstanding example of architectural and landscape beauty.

A large variety of outstanding trees have been used to beautify Chandigarh based on the above concepts. Illustrated here, along with photographs, are the salient features of some such trees. They show the structure, form, and texture. These are hardy and stand pollution abuse, are easy to grow and possess all qualities for making them suitable for city plantation.

Chukrasia tabularis commonly known as modern Neem, is one of the most exceptional features in this city. This tree has got all the superior qualities which make it as an ideal tree for almost all types of city roads. The photographs of this tree planted around Jan Marg (V2), sector dividing roads (V3), shopping streets (V4), circulation roads within sectors (V5) as well as access roads to dwellings (V6) of Chandigarh clearly demonstrate that this tree develops an excellent, tall straight trunk and a large crown of branches and foliage. The structure and roof-like top provides the right amount of shade and light to the entire space between buildings and roads. The tree meets the essential requirements of scale, structure and density of foliage. Its foliage is transparent and adds brilliance to the space.

3.12 Jan Marg (V2) road. Many rows of Chukrasia tree look splendid, added grandeur to the city. Plantation of Vikas Marg (V2) road too has been done with Chukrasia tree.

3.13 Sector dividing road (V3) - 100 feet wide. Chukrasia tree developed gorgeous green cover on the entire road.

3.14 Shopping street (V4) 44 feet wide in Sector 9. Chukrasia tree looks amazing. It is good for road as well as parking spaces.

3.15 Circulation road (V5) 60 feet wide in Sector 23. Provides wonderful roof of branches and foliage on the road as well as pedestrian path.

3.16 Road to dwellings (V6) in Silver City Urban Estate. Close plantation of Chukrasia tree on narrow road look innovative. (Trees are 4 years old)

Sweitenia macrophylla (Mahagony) has been planted around two 100 ft. wide important city roads called Udyog Path and Shanti Path. The photograph of the grand avenues created on these roads shows that this is a large structured tree, develops tall straight trunk, spreading crown and creates a beautiful roof of branches and foliage. These distinctive characteristics make it very suitable for city plantation. The use of only this tree along one avenue has helped create homogeneity of structure, texture and pattern. Both these major roads look perfect from a design standpoint and are very impressive. The trees could have been planted a little closer to the road curb to provide a good cover but they manage to provide a reasonable amount of cover to the entire space.

3.17 Udyog Path and Shanti Path - 100 feet wide sector roads. Mahagony tree plantation looks exciting. Trees developed green roof on the entire road.

Neem is the most outstanding tree for all kinds of wide and narrow roads of the city. It was extensively used by Luteyens for New Delhi roads. The photographs of the tree growing on circulation roads of Sector 22 (V5) shows grand dimensions, excellent pattern of branch structures and transparent crown due to which it provides the required amount of light to the entire space. Although the tree has been planted far away from the road curb yet it has provided green cover on the entire 60 feet wide road. This tree is ideal for all types of narrow and wide roads of the city.

3.18 Circulation road 60 feet wide (V5) Sector 22. Neem trees (Azadirachta indica) planted at a wide spacing of 30-40 feet. Trees take many years to fill up the spaces.

3.19 Circulation road (V5) 60 feet wide in Sector 22. Plantation of Neem tree (Azadirachta indica)looks gorgeous despite plantation carried out far away from road curb and pedestrian path.

Schleichera oleosa (Kusum) is another very functional and attractive tree that decorates city roads. Himalaya Marg which is 100 ft. wide road having 44' metalled portion has been exclusively planted with this tree. Photographs of this tree show its grand dimensions. This tree is structurally strong and big. The only challenge is that it has a tendency of branching at low height. This can be overcome by training and removing unwanted branches and the trunk and crown of the tree can be developed to the desired size and height. The most striking quality of this tree is that its foliage changes colours, from dark green to brilliant shades of red and yellow. Despite the fact that this tree has been planted at a good distance of 10 feet from the road curb, it completely covers the entire space between buildings and road with branches and foliage. Moreover, due to the use of single kind of tree on this road there is homogeneity of structure, texture and pattern that is visually very appealing.

3.20 Himalaya Marg - 100 feet wide (V3) road. Kusum trees (Schleichera oleosa) look spectacular in spite of the fact that plantation done at wide spacing of more than 30 feet and away from road curb.

3.21 Himalaya Marg, Chandigarh. Entire foliage of Kusum trees (Schleichera oleosa) becomes yellow in autumn months.

3.22 Himalaya Marg, Chandigarh. Entire foliage of Kusum trees (Schleichera oleosa) becomes brilliant red in spring season.

Bischofia javanica is another very functional and attractive tree that has been introduced for landscaping Chandigarh city roads and parks. A photograph of this tree planted on the wide V5 circulation road of Sector 7, 9, 33 shows the large size of the tree with a fairly tall, straight trunk and beautiful crown. These V5 roads are about 60 feet wide which gives a sense of how large this tree can grow. Bischofia is very suitable for plantation around all kinds of wide and narrow roads. The foliage of the crown is transparent and more uniformly distributed and permits lot of light and shade. It is also a very clean tree and its foliage does not litter the town.

3.23 Circulation road (V5) 60 feet wide in Sector 33. Masterful addition of amazing Bischofia tree (Bischofia javanica) added lot of beauty to the city. It is a neat large structured tree - does not spread litter.

Kigelia pinnata, another suitable tree for Chandigarh has been planted as an avenue around the main Sector road that divides Sector 22 & sector 23. The photograph of this road shows that being large structured, this tree has developed a strong trunk and expansive crown that has enhanced the urban elements providing green cover on almost the entire space between buildings and roads.

3.24 Main sector road (V3) - 100 feet wide dividing Sector 22 and 23. Pure single tree avenue of Kigelia pinnata developed glorious green ceiling on the entire road space.

Terminalia bellirica (Bahera) is another excellent tree that is structurally large and very suitable for wide, city roads. The photograph of the avenue planted along the 60 feet wide circulation (V5) road of Sector 36 shows the grand dimensions of this tree. It has a good pattern of straight trunk, branch structures and fairly transparent spreading crown. This tree is very suitable for all kind of city roads with a width of up to 200 feet. A single tree is capable of providing green cover for more than 30 feet of space. This avenue planted with only one kind of tree species has created an aesthetic visual homogencity of structure, texture and pattern.

3.25 Circulation road (V5) - 60 feet wide in Sector 36. Plantation of Bahera tree (Terminalia bellirica) looks spectacular. Tree develops tall straight trunk, excellent crown and provides wonderful green cover on entire road space. Suitable for wide city roads.

Another good tree planted on city roads and in parks is Alstonia schloris (Scholar tree). The glory of this tree lies in its outstanding functional and aesthetic value. The photograph shows the plantation on Vidya Path on the dividing road (V3) of Sector 36 and 37. The road is 100 feet wide with about 44 feet that is in metal. This tree is structurally very big also with a tall, strong trunk and spreading crown. This tree, like the Kusum has a tendency to develop too many branches at a low height and, therefore needs to be kept in shape by regular pruning. It can be groomed into attaining the desired effect with a tall, single trunk and canopy top.

3.26 Vidya Path (V3) -100 feet wide road dividing Sector 36 and 37. Scholar tree (Alstonia schloris) developed fabulous structures. Tree produces numerous branches on the trunk and need training.

Pterospermum acerifolium (Kanak Champa) is another functional tree that has been planted around city roads. The photograph shows one of the most impressive city avenues planted on the circulation (V5) road of Sector 37. It shows the massive structure of the tree with its tall, straight trunk, spreading crown and its ability to provide green cover on the large space of the road. Kanak Champa is also one of the trees that meet the functional requirements of scale, height and spread of tree structure as well as branch pattern and density of foliage.

3.27 Circulation road (V5) - 60 feet wide in Sector 37. Kanak Champa (Pterospermum acerifolium) develops tall straight trunks; spreading crowns provide excellent green cover on the entire road space. Does not obstruct views of the city. Good for wide and narrow roads.

3.28 Circulation road (V5) 60 feet wide, Sector 37. Kanak Champa (Pterospermum acerifolium) avenue planted at wide spacing of 30-40 feet. Takes several decades to fill up spaces.

Hardwickia binnata (Anjan) is one of the most functional, hardy and handsome trees which is a prized addition to the Chandigarh landscape. It is structurally large with an attractive trunk, crown and foliage. Photograph of the tree on 60 feet wide circulation road (V5) of Sector 22 shows the beauty and personality of this thee. The photograph shows that the tree has suffered some mutilation to compensate for the overhead electric installations.

3.29 Circulation road (V5) -60 feet wide in Sector 22. Hardwickia (Hardwickia binnata) is handsome tree having pretty structure, attractive pattern of branches and foliage. Tree is mutilated due to wrong installation of electric power lines.

The photograph of Vidya Path avenue shows the plantation of Haplophragma adenophyllum (Marod Phali). Homogeneous plantation of this single tree along this road has helped create a good look. It is an important sector dividing V3 road on which the major educational institutes of the city, namely, Punjab Engineering College, PGI and Panjab University are located.

Marod Phali is a large structure tree capable of developing tall, straight trunk and functional crown. Tree has been planted at a wide spacing of more than 30 feet from plant to plant and at a good distance from the road berm. It is a strong, hardy and durable tree that stands abuse from environmental pollution of the city. The one drawback is that its growth rate is very slow. This avenue is about 60 years old and as is evident from the picture the tree has not grown enough to provide a cover for the entire road space.

3.30 Vidya Path (V3) -100 feet wide road dividing Sector 14 and 15. Single kind of species of Marod Phali tree (Haplophragma adenophyllum) looks gorgeous. It is exceedingly slow growing tree and did not provide cover on entire road space even in six decades.

Mitragyna pariflora (Kaim) is a large structured and very tough, durable tree. It is growing in Sector 16 on the Madhya Marg around the slip road. The photograph of this avenue shows the dimensions of the tree, pattern of branches, density of foliage and its healthy growth. This tree is fairly suitable for various sizes of roads but has a relatively slow growth rate.

3.31 Slow carriage approach road to Multi Specialty Hospital located on Madhya Marg, Sector16. Plantation of Mitragyna tree (Mitragyna parviflora) on (V6) -40 feet wide road looks spectacular

Sarovar Path and Udyan Path are two important roads of the city. Both are 100 feet wide with a 44 foot metalled portion. The only exceptionally large sized tree that has been planted on these roads is the Ficus infectoria (Pilkhan). The picture of the avenue shows that this tree does not have a tall, straight trunk. The tree has a strong tendency to develop extensive unwanted growth of thick structured side branches which develop at a fairly low height. Also, the tree forms a dense spreading crown that tends to block the distant views of the city. So, this tree too needs to be groomed and unwanted branch growth from the trunk of the tree has to be removed to bring the crown to the desired height.

3.32 Udyan Path - 100 feet wide (V3) road, Sector 24. Ficus infectoria does not develop tall, straight trunk, narrowed the road space, blocks architectural views.

3.33 Udyan Path and Sarovar Path -100 feet wide sector dividing (V3) roads. Ficus infectoria (Pilkhan) has been planted on both these important roads. Trees blocked architectural views of the city, reduced road spaces and sunlight. Inherently this tree develops low trunks and extensive unmanageable crowns, cause obstruction in movement of traffic. Now trees need drastic pruning of limbs for raising crowns to desired height.

Multi-storey buildings and sky scrapers in the commercial centre of Sector 17 are accented by very tall species of trees called Sterculia alata and Eucalyptus citriodora. Both these kinds are very suitable and harmonize exceedingly well around high buildings. Photographs of these tree plantations show the dimensions i.e. height and spread, as well as structure of the tree, their branches and density of foliage etc. They develop very tall trunks and narrow spreading crowns suitable for narrow roads which subdue the effect of massive building structures.

3.34 Double carriage road around multistoried commercial city centre, Sector 17. Tall Eucalyptus citriodora trees look gorgeous. Massive concrete buildings have been subdued with big structures of trees having exquisite crowns and low density foliage.

3.35 City Road in commercial central Sector 17. Closely planted (Eucalyptus citriodora) trees develop tall straight trunk narrow high crown, do not obstruct view of the city, and fill up spaces in shortest period.

4

IMPORTANT CHANDIGARH CITY ROADS: OPPORTUNITIES FOR IMPROVEMENT

CHANDIGARH undeniably has many outstanding kinds of trees suitable for roadside plantation. As we study their features and the benefits they bring to city streets, there is also an opportunity to highlight some aspects that can be improved.

A detailed study of some of the important roads of Chandigarh that can use the improvement is presented here. As this need is recognized and acknowledged, the problems can be addressed by re-planting on these roads for lasting beautification.

The Chandigarh city roads discussed here are:

1. Uttar Marg

2. Vigyan Marg

3. Jan Marg

4. Madhya Marg

5. Dakshan Marg

4.1 A view of Uttar Marg shows numerous kinds of trees planted haphazardly away from the road curb leaving the road devoid of green cover. The pedestrian path too is very close to the high speed vehicular traffic road.It can be moved in and trees planted closer to the road.

Uttar Marg

In Chandigarh this avenue is important as it divides the entire city from the City Capitol Complex. The area is strategic in its location with some other important landmarks like the Lake Club, Rock Garden, MLA hostels and flats, Ministers' houses, the Bougainvillea Garden and Engineering College. On the eastern side of the road is located the popular tourist attraction, Sukhna Lake. This road is 150 feet wide of which 44 feet is metalled .

As we examine the finer details of the planting here, we observe that the entire plantation on this road is haphazard. It has a collection of 37 kinds of small and big trees, and almost 15 varieties of shrubs that have been used. Also, the trees are planted at a large distance away from the road. There is about a 110 foot wide area that is available for beautification, which should allow about 5 rows of trees planted approximately 20 feet apart from each other. A lush green cover over the entire 150 foot wide road space, 44 feet of which is mettaled, can be created by using a single kind of large structured trees. The tree trunks can form large crowns creating a scenic view of the Kasauli hills as well as the buildings of the Capitol Complex i.e. the Secretariat, Assembly building and High Court. One can imagine that a beautiful green tunnel effect of 150 feet can create to make to a beautiful place to visit!

4.2 A side view of the 110 foot space along Uttar Marg. This too shows the numerous kinds of small structured trees planted haphazardly.

4.3 Another view of Uttar Marg taken from the interior shows the wide 110 foot space with trees and shrubs planted in an irregular manner. It demonstrates how random plantation can ruin a large space that otherwise can be planted correctly to make it an important landscape feature of the city.

4.4 Another view of Uttar Marg shows several varieties of trees with different structures and planted far away from the road curb.

Below is a presentation of an ideal road plantation pattern for a 150 foot wide road. It shows five rows of single kind of large structured trees planted on the 110 foot wide side of the road and a single row on the other side of the metalled road. The trees are planted at a spacing of 20 feet from tree to tree and row to row.

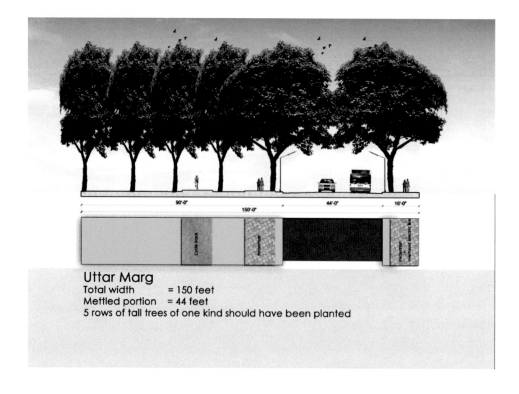

Uttar Marg
Total width   = 150 feet
Mettled portion   = 44 feet
5 rows of tall trees of one kind should have been planted

Vigyan Marg

Vigyan Marg is an important city road running from sectors 2 to 6 on the north and dividing sectors 7 to 11 on the south. The prominent landmarks on this road are the Chandigarh Golf Course, Punjab Raj Bhawan, the Leisure Valley, the MLA Hostels/flats and the Punjab Engineering College. It is a V3 road with a 33 foot wide metalled portion.

This road has been planted with 27 different kinds of trees that has led to some visual disorderliness. There is an opportunity here to create a harmonious look by repetitive planting of same species of trees.

Overhead electric power lines have been installed on the road curb in front of the row of trees which has left no space for the growth of trees.

This major road can be planned and replanted. A single kind of large structured tree species should be used which will bring about homogeneity. The trees should be planted close to the road curb, pedestrian paths and electric installations should be behind the trees.. An excellent plantation pattern has been prepared, which if adopted can bring outstanding results.

Below is an ideally designed view of the tree plantation pattern of Vigyan Marg. It shows plantation of two rows of single kind of large structured trees planted on either side of the 33-feet- wide metalled road, close to the verge. The pedestrian passage and overhead electric power lines have been installed away from the row of trees. This ensures that the crowns of the trees get adequate space for development to be able to provide and a grand green canopy of trees structure, branches and foliage on the entire road. Trees are planted closely spaced, 15 feet from plant to plant so that they develop straight tall trunks and fill up the road space in a short period of time.

4.6 A view of a portion of road dividing Sector 2 and 11 shows small structured flowering trees planted away from the road curb leaving the metalled portion of the road without any green cover.

4.7 Another view of the road taken on the portion of the road dividing Sector 5 and 8. The photograph shows overhead power lines installed adjoining the road curb in a disorderly manner. The different species of trees planted far apart has not left any space for the development of their crowns leading to a messy look.

4.8 Another view of Vigyan Path shows numerous species of trees with variable structures and irregular pattern of branches, foliage and texture. The plantation is far away from road curb. Overhead power lines are installed too close to the road. They look unattractive and because the trees are planted very close behind them, the tree crowns have had to be mutilated to avoid damage that could cause power disruption.

4.9 This view of Vigyan Path again poorly planted areas with diverse species, structures and patterns of trees not providing the necessary green cover to the metalled road.

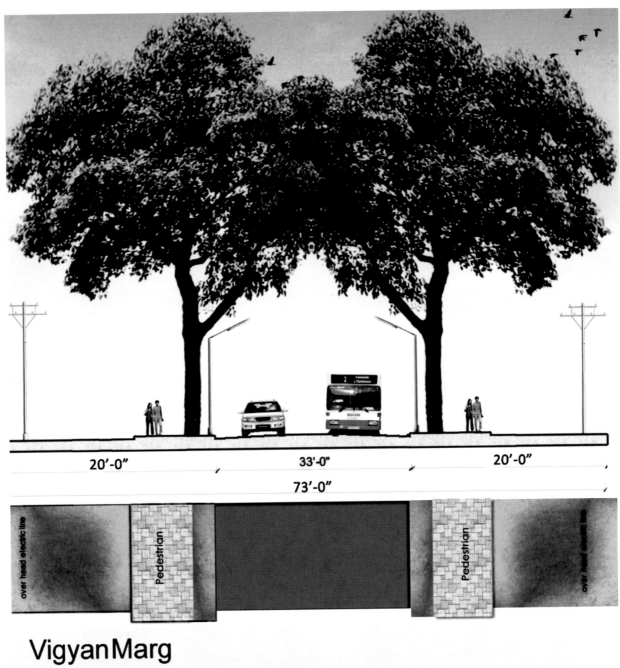

VigyanMarg

Total Width   = 73 Feet
Mettled Portion = 33 Feet
Lanes   = 3 no's

Jan Marg

Jan Marg runs north to south, dividing the city into two parts. It is the main road that runs in the middle of the city with major attractions on either sides, Sector 17 city center, Rose Garden, the Museum, Chandigarh Secretariat and Punjab Mini Secretariat. It is the approach road to the Capitol Complex. It also has the 2 large 5-star hotel properties, The Taj and Shivalik View.

This avenue has a double-carriage 330 foot wide road including the metalled part, green belt and a 6 foot central verge. There is also a green belt alongside the road for tree plantation.

This road has been planted with 20 varieties of trees and yet the desired effect of quality landscaping has not been achieved Ideally 13 rows in all, six on either side and one in the centre could have been planted to create a great visual effect. Similar kind of trees can be planted at a spacing of 20 feet from row to row and plant to plant. Tall, straight trunk trees can be planted to facilitate clearer and broader views. A wonderful green ceiling of tree branches can be created on the entire metalled road giving a tunnel like look with arched canopies. A green cover also helps keep the roads cool in summer and warm in winter.

An ideal view presenting a magnificent plantation pattern of the entire 330 feet wide Jan Marg is presented below. It shows the plantation of 13 rows of one single kind of large structured trees. Six rows are planted on each side and one row in the divider at spacing of 20 feet from tree to tree and row to row. Plantation has been shown close to the road verges.

4.11 This picture is the view of Jan Marg between Sector 16 and 17 showing multiple rows of trees planted on either sides on this 135 foot wide green belt. The view of the road shows that trees have been planted far away from the road curb. There are no trees on central divider either due to which both sides of the road are without a green cover.

4.12 A side view of Jan Marg also shows tree plantation done far away from the road curb. Hence, even though numerous rows of trees have been planted; the required objective of creating green ceiling on the road has not been realized.

4.13 Another view of Jan Marg shows different species of trees planted due to which the desired impact of quality landscaping has not been created . Another noticeable mistake is that the main road on the side of Sector 17 has been punctured. A slow carriage way and parking has been provided , compromising the concept of providing a 135 foot green belt on either side of Jan Marg.

4.14 A vast portion of Jan Marg alongside Sector 10 (on the left) shows numerous small structured trees. These have tilted trunks and are not very suitable for roadside plantation. The side along Sector 9 (on the rigth) shows numerous gaps of trees as well as a mixture of different species of trees. The photograph also shows the slow carriage way and parking areas that have been constructed on the side of Sector 9, against the original concept of developing Jan Marg with extensive plantation of the beautiful large structured trees.

4.15 Another view of Jan Marg photographed from Sectors 3 and 4 shows the metalled road without any green cover because the trees have been planted far away from the road verge.

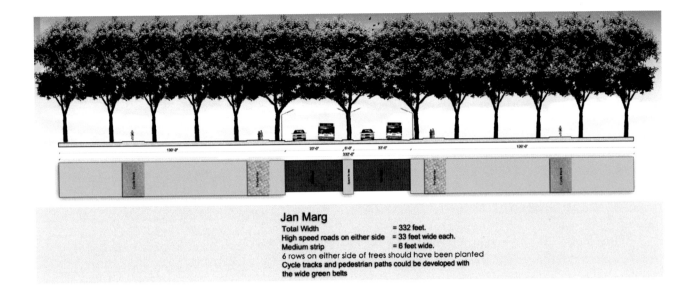

Jan Marg
Total Width = 332 feet.
High speed roads on either side = 33 feet wide each.
Medium strip = 6 feet wide.
6 rows on either side of trees should have been planted
Cycle tracks and pedestrian paths could be developed with
the wide green belts

Madhya Marg

This is the most important road in Chandigarh, dividing the city into the northern and southern sectors. It is also the road that connects the city to Punjab, leading into Siswan and Ropar on the one side and , Haryana into Panchkula and onwards into Shimla, Himachal Pardesh on the other. Sector 17, the commercial center of the city is located on this road. Other important attractions include the Rose Garden, the Government College for Men, the Government College for Girls, the General Hospital, the PGI and Panjab University. Other major commercial areas, Bhawans, prominent fruit-vegetable market and timber market also are alongside this major road.

The Madhya Marg is a double carriage road, 240 feet wide with a 33 feet metalled portion on either of the 4 foot wide central verge. There are two slow carriage-ways 22 feet wide on either side of the main road with four 18 feet wide green verges.

For a road of this importance the Madhya Marg is not adequately planted. It certainly does not reflect Chandigarh as the well planned and landscaped city it is so well known for. There are 27 species of trees planted on this road creating a haphazard look. Trees have been planted so far away from the road that almost the entire 66 feet wide sides of the main carriage-way are deprived of green cover. There is a great opportunity to create uniformity and brilliant views by replanting. Large structured trees with similar growth patterns and texture would greatly enhance the look of this high visibility, heavy traffic road. Also, there is room to plant about six rows of trees spaced 15 feet from each other and between rows to make a significant impact. This with the well planted parking areas will help provide complete green cover and the desired shade in summers and light in winters.

4.17 This view of Madhya Marg between Sectors 7 and 19 shows that it is a double carriage road. It is planted with a mixture of different structurally sized species of trees. Some are small, and do not meet the scale requirements. Others that are medium or large sized are kept too low, not giving the desired visual effect. This photograph also shows that the central verge is without trees leaving the entire road including slow carriage ways and parking areas without the required green cover.

4.18 Another view of Madhya Marg shows low trunks and crowns that have not been raised to the required height.

4.19 This view of the approach road to Madhya Marg from Panchkula is absolutely treeless and bare. Overhead electric power lines have been installed very close to the road berm without leaving any space for tree plantation. The large central divider too is without any trees.

4.20 Another view of the approach road to Madhya Marg from the railway station of the city also shows a bare, treeless road. Overhead electric power lines too are installed without any planning. This is heavily used approach road and a major entry point into the city Uncountable people come to the city on this road which carries the first impression of this city. The city is now six decades old yet no effort has been made to beautify the approach to this city. A huge parking area in front of railway station is also absolutely treeless.

4.21 Photograph showing a small portion of a slow carriage way of Madhya Marg which has been planted with one kind of large structured tree. It is an approach road to the General Hospital in Sector 16. This 22 feet wide little carriage way is demonstration of exemplary tree planting work. It is an example of how all of the Madhya Marg, other main roads, slow carriage-ways and parking areas be planted.

A view of a good tree plantation pattern that should be adopted for plantation of Madhya Marg is demonstrated below. The road section shows five rows of very large structured trees of only one kind planted at a spacing of 15 feet from plant to plant in straight rows. Madhya Marg planted in this way with wonderful tall trunks of trees with excellent spreading crowns will add grandeur to this important road and the entire city.

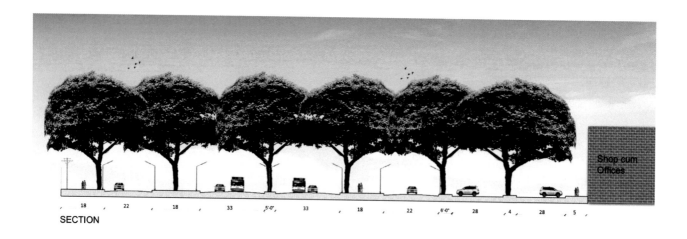

SECTION

PLAN

Madhya Marg

Total Width	= 240 Feet
Mettled Portion	= 33 Feet + 33 Feet
	(double carriage)
	= 3 lanes on either side
Slow Carriage	= 22 Feet + 22 Feet
	2 Lanes on either side

Dakshan Marg

Dakshan Marg is not only the approach road from New Delhi, this road also connects several important towns of Punjab and Haryana. All the long-route buses follow this road starting at the Chandigarh International airport, along The Tribune building the commercial hub in Sector 34, Government Medical College and Hospital in Sector 32, and other major commercial areas of the city.

It is a 184 feet wide road with a double 33 feet wide metalled carriage-way on either side. There is a 5 feet center verge and two slow carriage vehicular roads of 22 feet on both sides of the high speed road. The slow carriage-way and the high speed road have green belts 22 feet wide as well as 12 feet wide berms on either side. There are 19 varieties of trees on this road that have been at varying distances from each other and not the standard, specified spacing of 15 feet between trees and between rows. This major artery can be re planted as well, with large trunked trees with high, full crowns allowing for necessary greenery on the entire road.

A perfect view of the tree plantation design for Dakshan Marg is demonstrated below. It shows the plantation of five rows of large structured trees planted at a spacing of 15 feet from plant to plant. Only one kind of tree with a tall, straight trunk, a vast spreading crown and attractive evergreen foliage is planted on the entire road.

4.23 This view of Dakshan Marg taken at the entry point to the city shows the road that was planted 60 years ago. It demonstrates that even after a long 6 decade period the desired green cover on the road has not been achieved. This is due to the same reasons that have been highlighted earlier, no trees on the central verge and trees alongside the road planted far away from the road curb. Tree trunks too are left very low hence not creating an attractive visual impact.

4.24 Another view of Dakshan Marg shows the numerous gaps in tree plantation. Most of the road is treeless. Only one, unplanned tree planted in the central divider is not serving any purpose.

4.25 Photograph of Dakshan Marg taken between Sector 23 and 36 is another view of the same poor practices that have kept the road from having an attractive green cover.

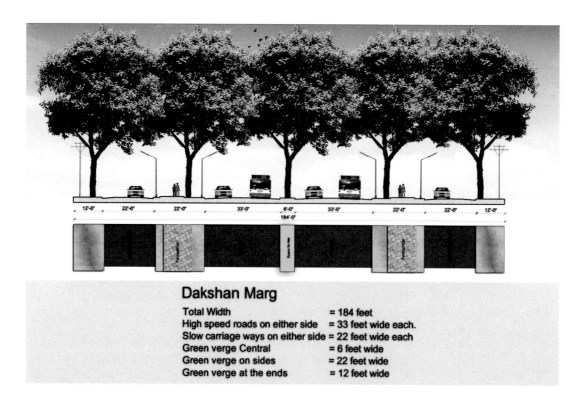

Dakshan Marg

Total Width	= 184 feet
High speed roads on either side	= 33 feet wide each.
Slow carriage ways on either side	= 22 feet wide each
Green verge Central	= 6 feet wide
Green verge on sides	= 22 feet wide
Green verge at the ends	= 12 feet wide

In Summary

The original city plans provided for use of specific trees for each of the five important roads in Chandigarh. However, most of the species that were selected did not perform as desired, leaving gaps that have been filled over time with diverse species. This has led to haphazard growth of trees along major roads. Uttar Marg, for example was originally planted with Erythrines and Bottle palm trees. Since neither of these did well, these were replaced with 37 different kinds of species. Similarly, Vigyan Marg, was planted with flowering species like Millettias, Spathodeas and other such species that did not do well and were replaced with a mixed species of trees.

Same was the case with Dakshan Marg that now has 19 different species and Jan Marg with 20 species. Similarly, Madhya Marg was originally planted with Grevillea robustas and Jacarandas that failed over the span of 20 years. Now there are 27 species of trees that make up this major avenue. Some of these, like Cassia Siamea are brittle and end up causing damage to vehicles and accidents on this busy road.

Another issue to highlight is that the city was planned by Le Corbusier to have roads running north-south and east-west This positioning of roads leads to problems related to vehicular traffic as a result of the position of the sun at certain times of the day. This can be accommodated by appropriate tree plantation. While this was planned for as the city was conceived and built it was not executed in entirety. Tree plantation in Chandigarh has been done specifically in relation to the orientation of the sun. There are two directions of roads. The vertical roads are parallel to the avenue of the Capitol and horizontal roads are parallel to Madhya Marg. All the vertical and horizontal roads of the city create a challenge for the morning and evening hours vehicular traffic in winter when the sun is low on the horizon and therefore straight in the eyes. This makes it essential to provide adequate green cover on roads. Where we have not executed correctly is in the selection of trees used, plantation not done close to roads and the trees not allowed to reach the desired height.

Apart from the main roads discussed above, the approach roads from the Chandigarh Railway station, the Airport and Mohali need to be improved too. As we discuss roads extensively, we must keep in mind that large open parking areas such as the Railway station, Sector 17 plaza and others that are largely devoid of suitable trees, need to be appropriately planted. This is well demonstrated by all the photographs showing the lack of appropriate use of our rich local tree bank.

There is a great opportunity to improve the landscaping of city roads and an absolute need for re-planting some of the roads discussed here not only to rectify these mistakes but also to plan ahead to provide a beautiful habitat and picturesque greenery in the city and also to counter the growing effects of pollution in the city.

5

FUNDAMENTAL REQUIREMENTS OF TREE PLANTATION

THERE are a few essential elements in creating an ideal tree plantation design for urban areas. The fundamental considerations of effective urban tree selection and plantation are :

1. Structure and texture of the tree

2. Density of tree plantation - including shape and form

3. Diversity - avoiding mixtures of many kinds

4. Use of flowering trees

5. Arranging trees - formally or informally

6. Scale

7. Plantation close to the road curb.

STRUCTURE AND TEXTURE OF THE TREE

Structure of the tree is the most important factor for creating an excellent design with trees for urban plantation. Large trees develop a tall straight trunk and upright high branched crown that provides an attractive look. Wide spreading trees do not develop tall straight trunks and high spreading crowns.

Big structured trees enhance urban elements rather than hiding them. They adjust space vertically and create a ceiling with lot of variability in transparency and height. Due to their big structure, clearness at the pedestrian eye level permits the visual grasp of the extensive and broad areas of the city.

Sturdy, hardy, durable trees with big structure are very functional and can counter abuse from environmental pollution. Structurally large trees that meet aesthetic requirements, needing little care and maintenance and suitable to the local agro-climatic conditions are ideal for planting around city roads. Urban plantation done using such trees produces an excellent design and fills up entire spaces around city roads in the shortest possible time.

Large structured trees with a straight trunk, superior texture of branches, foliage and spreading crowns create outdoor greenrooms; produce wonderful environment and excellent feeling of moving through them. They help create a uniform pattern of light and shade on the street. They are most effective and healthy if grown close enough together for their branches to intermingle and create very strong network. Large trees not only look good but also are useful and functional.

Another important fact is that all kinds of large structured trees naturally have very deep root systems due to which there is no danger of them getting uprooted due to storms or any other environmental hazards. The deep roots also prevent any damage to underground services such as sewer, storm water, electric and underground drinking water lines.

5.1 Picture of Neem trees (Azadirachta indica) on Tees January Marg at New Delhi. The large structured trees have developed tall, straight trunks and excellent crowns that have modulated the entire space vertically and created a grand, textured green ceiling on the entire road. The big structure helps create transparency at the pedestrian eye level and a visual grasp of extensive and broad areas in the city.

5.2 Mahagony trees (Swietenia macrophylla) planted in Chandigarh on Udyog Marg on the road dividing sectors 16 and 23. Here too, large structured trees have developed excellent high trunks and spreading crowns. The entire metalled road space is filled up with green, attractive, high branched, crown bearing, dark green nicely textured foliage.

DENSITY OF TREE PLANTATION - INCLUDING SHAPE AND FORM

Density of tree plantation in urban areas is another important consideration that contributes to the creation of aesthetic greening of a city in a short period of time.

Trees spaced wide apart take several years to fill up the urban spaces and do not create the required impact on the scale of the street even in a long period of over 50 years. Widely spaced trees never make a good pattern and take many years to form an arched canopy that is needed to achieve visual unity. Close tree plantation can create a tight visual link in a fairly short period of time.

5.4 Close planting on a V4 road has allowed trees to develop tall, straight trunks and narrow high crown keeping them from obstructing views of architectural structures in the city.

The discipline of urban design emphasizes the use of trees to accentuate architectural structures and not to hide the structures of the city. Trees grown at wider spaces produce low branched crowns that not only obstruct broad architectural views of the city but also occupy lot of street space, making roads narrow obstructing the movement of traffic. Low-branched spreading crowns also restrict sunlight and create gloominess.

There is a notion that trees planted too close are not as healthy as those grown at wide spacing. This is incorrect. The fact is that open grown trees are much more susceptible to injury and disease. Trees that are grown close to each other are healthier. Planting trees close together allows branches to intermingle and create a very strong network of the crown that in turn gives strength to the trunk of the tree.

5.3 Photograph shows Terminalia bellirica closely planted around the circulation road in Sector 36. This plantation has filled up the entire space making a continuous arched canopy and creating appropriate impact on the scale of the street, in a short period of time.

This concept of closely planting trees has not been adopted either in Lutyens' New Delhi as well as Corbusier's Chandigarh, famously known for being the best planned cities in India. In Delhi, trees have been planted 30 to 40 feet apart due to which it has taken over 80 years for the trees to develop complete personality and fill up spaces on roads. In Chandigarh too, after 60 years the desired objective has not been achieved. Despite the fact that tree plantation received high priority and was done with lot of planning and thought, the outcome in both these cities has not been as impactful due to this very lapse in design and approach.

5.6 This photograph shows widely spreading trees that have not developed tall straight trunks or high spreading crowns. Such low branched crowns obstruct broad architectural views and cause obstruction in the movement of traffic.

Shape of trees has been another major concept adopted for city plantation in Chandigarh. Shape, in fact has no significance in urban plantation and should not have been a consideration. Shape of trees is greatly altered by the space in which they are planted. The reality is that trees can grow at any possible spacing. Genetic evolution in fact, favours tree plantation in close groups and there is no biological basis for keeping trees far apart. Trees in urban areas, around roads as well as open spaces and parks should be planted no more than 15 feet apart.

5.5 These are 4-year old trees. Because they have been planted very close together they have created aesthetically beautiful greening in a very short period of time.

5.7 This is a photograph of a road in Lutyens' New Delhi demonstrating trees planted 30 to 40 feet apart. Due to this it has taken over 80 years for New Delhi roads to develop the real effect and fill up entire space on the roads.

5.8 Photograph shows how the tree planted far away at wide spacing in Lutyens' New Delhi roads developed low spreading crowns which were raised to the required level in many decades after plantation.

5.9 Photograph shows widely spaced trees on V3 roads in Chandigarh that fail to provide the necessary green cover on the road even after 60 years.

5.10 This is a demonstration of the importance given to shape of the tree in city plantation in Chandigarh.

DIVERSITY - AVOID MIXING TREE SPECIES

A very important requirement in creating an excellent design is the use of only one kind of tree at a specific site. Single kind of tree species planted on each city street helps in unifying individual parts into a single whole. The homogeneity of structure, texture, pattern, light and shade that comes from using same kinds of trees creates a fantastic collective impact as opposed to mixing up too many species which results a haphazard look and damages the quality of landscape of a city.

Lutyens applied this concept on planting New Delhi roads. He created a wonderful model that should be adopted in the entire country wherever planned urban habitats are being developed.

In Chandigarh too, single kind of species were planted on most of the roads. However, over time this has changed for several other reasons that will be addressed later in the book. As a result some important roads have too many varieties of trees that have damaged the quality of landscape of this city. A large mix of trees has also been used in parks, open spaces and around public buildings in Chandigarh that has marred the overall landscape design of the city.

5.11 View of Tughlak road in New Delhi shows the plantation of single kind of tree species creating an attractive look. The homogeneity of structure, texture and pattern, enhances the beauty on the city. Lutyens planted all roads in New Delhi using single kind of tree species.

5.12 View of an avenue planted with the same Kigelia pinnata trees on V3 road in Chandigarh. The uniform structure and pattern has produced excellent design. In Chandigarh too, most city roads have been planted with single kind of tree species.

USE OF FLOWERING TREES

Flowering trees are primarily used in urban areas to add colour to city landscape. However, that cannot be the only criteria for tree selection. There are many compelling reasons for why using flowering species for plantation on city roads is unsuitable.

First, flowering tree species are structurally very small. They never grow large enough to create the desired tall straight trunks and effective crown that are needed for city roads.

Secondly, the blooming period of most flowering trees is very short. It ranges from 2 to 4 weeks in a year which is when they provide glorious colour. For the remaining 48 to 50 weeks, they are without flowers and not serving the desired purpose.

Third, most flowering kinds of trees do not have dense foliage and hence do not provide enough shade. Also, because they are structurally small, they never fill up the entire space planned and provided between buildings and roads in the city. They do not develop continuous arched canopies and do not create the desired visual unity.

Finally, flowering trees are short lived and are difficult to grow and maintain.

Irrespective of all the drawbacks flowering trees have in urban plantation they have been planted extensively in Chandigarh on almost all roads including major roads, Uttar Marg, Vigyan Marg, Madhya Marg and Capital avenue. Flowering trees such as Gulmohur, Jacarandas, and several kinds of Legerstroemias, Cassias and Bauhinias have been planted on the shopping streets in Chandigarh. The intent in using them was to give character and a unique identity to the shopping area of each sector. Several species of flowering trees have also been planted around all the circulation roads and access roads to residential areas in every sector.

5.17 Photograph shows flowering trees, small in size and structure. Their blooming period is very small and they are short lived and also difficult to grow and maintain.

ARRANGING TREES - FORMALLY OR INFORMALLY

Trees in urban habitat can be arranged either formally in straight rows and geometric patterns or in a free form, natural informal.

All planned urban development in cities and towns is created in formal patterns. Roads, buildings and all structures are planned formally in straight lines in geometric and regular grid patterns. Therefore, it is only appropriate to arrange trees in a similar fashion, formally in straight rows and geometric pattern so that they harmonize with other structural components of a city.

All types of trees, shrubs and other plants used for landscaping in the urban habitat are natural. So, even if they are arranged in a regular and formal manner in straight lines and rectangular grids throughout the city, the effect created will be natural and hence

5.13 View of the Uttar Marg shows mixture of many kinds of species which look haphazard and has damaged the quality of landscape.

5.14 View of a park in Sector 9 Chandigarh shows random plantation of several kinds of trees which looks disorderly.

5.15 Another view of a park in sector 7, Chandigarh showing haphazard plantation.

informal. They will create beautiful 'spaces' and look attractive as every tree or shrub of a different structure and pattern will make each formal space look unique.

Formal designs are based on rational planning, imagination and expression of human creativity which result in orderly setting of plants, producing clarity, proportion, rhythm, balance and harmony. The informal tradition is generally recognized as having greater vitality than formal setting. This is because informal tradition is derived from nature. In this tradition, regularity, geometry, straight lines and the sharp corners etc. are totally rejected and setting of all the plant material is done in a natural manner which requires professional handling. Integrating and blending an informal setting with a formal plan for a lasting bond is an art. If not done right it may result in unorganized growth. Only a professional can create an ideal setting composed of formal and informal plant space. Not every practical gardener, nurseryman, park superintendent or any professional can do this work. In an effort to create an informal setting if a sprinkling of trees and shrubs is used indiscriminately it can ruin the landscape and create a confused, haphazard effect. The task of selecting, setting and composing formal and informal plant spaces should only be handled by professionals and not amateur gardeners.

5.16 View of Vigyan Marg planted with Millettia ovalifolia flowering trees shows that these trees are structurally very small and do not meet scale requirements and hence are unsuitable for city road plantation.

5.18 View of a New Delhi road shows that the entire plantation has been done formally in straight lines in geometric and regular grid pattern.

5.19 View of a Chandigarh road planted formally in straight rows on geometric pattern also shows highly exciting and glorious pattern developed in this city.

Lutyens created the New Delhi Master Plan about 100 years ago. He designed the entire plantation of roads too. He developed an absolutely natural and informal pattern even though the trees have been planted formally in straight rows. It has been possible to achieve this because trees are natural materials that create spectacular views even when they are arranged in straight lines. The only need is to arrange their orderly setting keeping in view the fundamental requirements of their structure, density, diversity, and scale etc. Therefore there is no need to adopt informal settings in carrying out city's road plantation. The same concept can be adopted and practiced in developing city parks and special landscape gardens as well as for informal plantings around buildings and homes.

Similarly in Chandigarh, most of the V3's, the sector dividing roads have been planted in this manner. Roads look natural even though the trees have been planted in straight lines. Further the use of single kind plant having uniform structure, height, spread and pattern has added beauty.

SCALE

Scale and special proportions are other fundamental concerns for tree plantation in urban areas. Scale implies a relationship between dimensions of the tree and those of urban spaces as perceived by human beings. Most of the tree species that are small or medium sized do not meet the inherent scale requirements of city streets and are too small to create an arching cover of branches and foliage. Similarly, flowering varieties of trees which too are small in size cannot achieve the scale transition. They never grow large

enough to develop shady canopies that are needed for city streets. This is why public spaces in urban spaces especially around roads appear distractingly inappropriate and out of scale. Therefore, planting small scale trees in a city is conceptually against what the tree in the city could and should be. They make already narrow streets seem narrower and when planted in open spaces seem out of place. So, to enhance the look of narrow streets and make them look wide, tall trees should be planted.

Some of photographs showing plantation not done according to scale reveal the importance of scale in carrying out tree plantation in our urban habitat.

Most of Chandigarh city roads including shopping streets, circulation roads in various sectors as well as approach roads to dwellings are planted with small sized trees that do not meet the scale requirements. The fundamental need of meeting the appropriate relationship between dimensions of a tree and the space around roads and buildings is missing.

The lack of regard to scale and other tree plantation basics discussed is evident in the planned city of Panchkula. Small structured flowering trees have been planted around these roads. Trees are out of scale and are too small in size and will never grow large enough to develop shady canopies that are needed for city streets. The pedestrian paths have been provided adjacent to the fast speed roads. Electric power lines are installed along the line of trees.

5.20 Photograph shows Sector 10 side of Jan Marg which is an important V2 city road. A row of very small sized flowering trees have been planted that are distractingly inappropriate and totally out of scale. A road the size of Jan Marg needs large structured trees that would develop long trunks and spreading crowns to create a green cover on the entire road.

5.21 Photograph of Vigyan Marg between Sectors 2 and 11 is another example of plantation of very small structured flowering trees that are absolutely out of scale. These will always remain inherently small and never provide any green cover on this road.

5.22 Another view of a sector shopping center demonstrates the lack of attention to scale in tree plantation.

5.23 Photograph of an important double carriage high speed road in Panchkula. It demonstrates lack of use of the fundamental concepts of urban roads plantation i.e. no attention to scale, trees planted far from curb, trees planted at large distances from each other, different kinds of trees used on one avenue.

PLANTING CLOSE TO THE ROAD CURB

The principle of planting trees close to the curb is applicable to all types of streets in urban areas. When the trees reach maturity, the effect is spectacular. This is what has been done by Sir Lutyens in New Delhi.

The obvious benefit of planting large structured trees close to the curb is that the entire space on the road for vehicular and pedestrian traffic gets a much needed green cover, creating a wonderful effect on the scale of the streets.

In Chandigarh, Mohali and Panchkula, the major modern day planned urban towns, this concept has not been adopted. The trees are planted far away from the road curb and therefore, not providing the benefit the tree is expected to give. Also, the vehicular traffic and pedestrian pathways are built adjacent to each other putting the trees away from the road and the pedestrian way.

Additionally, overhead electric lines are installed right next to the trees. When trees grow upto the height of electric lines, the crowns of the trees are chopped off to maintain electric supply to city residents. Therefore, the entire effort made in growing trees around the roads goes waste. It is very essential that tree is given due respect in the city and right place is planned and provided for their proper growth in the cities.

Planting trees close to the road curb is important for the following reasons:
1) Trees develop continuous arched canopies due to which visual unity is achieved. It helps in unification and binding the spaces of the city together.
2) There is a clear visual and psychological separation between vehicular and pedestrian traffic.
3) Trees are very effective in providing shade to the street and the side walk.
4) The glare and heat of intense summer sun as well as sleet and blast of winters on the roads is reduced.

5.24 Tughlak road in New Delhi is a perfect example of the spectacular effect created by separating vehicular and pedestrian traffic with use of trees. The trees are providing shade to the entire road and the side walk.

5.25 Photograph of an important road in Chandigarh shows that the principle of planting trees close to the curb has not been adopted. Over head electric lines are installed without any plan and no pedestrian space has been provided.

5.26 A picture of one of Chandigarh's circulation road shows tree plantation done away from road curbs and vehicular traffic and space for pedestrian movement constructed along each. Overhead electric lines are also installed along the tree lines.

6

ADOPTING STANDARD ROAD CROSS-SECTIONS

ALL states across the country are governed by town planning laws. These laws enable town planning departments and urban local bodies to prepare master plans ensuring that cities are developed in an organized manner. Private entrepreneurs too are encouraged to develop layouts that are approved by appropriate local authorities. All kinds of basic infrastructure and public health amenities such as roads, sewerage systems, water and electric supply, pipe lines for drainage as well as traffic needs are planned and provided for quality urban living. However, tree plantation, a vital component for improving the environment of a city is ignored and not incorporated in the planning process.

Trees make the micro climate of a locale and help moderate it providing protection from extreme weather conditions, noise and air pollutants. Scientific studies show that trees cut off 69% of sun's heat from the ground which means that areas densely planted with trees are much cooler in summer and warmer in winter than non-planted areas. Trees also reduce wind velocity by 63% and reduce pollution due to dust fall by 66%. Trees reduce suspended particulate matter by 42% and noise by 50%. A single large tree is capable of producing about 5 tons of oxygen and can consume almost an equal amount of carbon-dioxide in a day. Thus, trees play a tremendous role in filtering the atmosphere and improving the physical environment of urban areas to make them livable. These are facts that reinforce the need for tree plantation as an integral part of a city plan.

6.1 Photograph of Vigyan Marg shows trees planted far away from the road verge and electric installations right next to the road. The road is devoid of any green cover.

6.2 View of Vigyan Marg road between Sector 5 and 8 showing overhead power lines installed on the road curb in front of the row of trees not leaving any space for the growth and development of trees.

In modern, planned cities such as Chandigarh, Mohali and Panchkula tree plantation is recognized as important but there is evidence of a lack of coordination with other infrastructural amenities that go into making an effectively planned city. This chapter focuses on the opportunity for better planning by showing some existing standard road cross sections and illustrates ideal cross-sections.

Almost every road in Chandigarh, Mohali or Panchkula is demonstrative of lack of planning across tree plantation, road and electric installations. Trees have been planted far back from the verge of the road. As a result there is no shade on the road. Electric installations have been installed right next to the road, leading to unsightly appearances and totally defeating the purpose of planting trees for beautification. All these concepts applied across this tri-city area are fundamentally against the basic principles of good urban landscaping.

6.4 Photograph showing a highly decorative Harwickia binnata tree on 60 feet wide V5 road in sector 22 totally mutilated due to the wrong installation of overhead power lines.

6.3 Photograph of Neem trees (Azadirachta indica) on V5 road in Sector 22 shows pedestrian path adjacent to the road.

6.5 Photograph of a fully grown Mahagony tree (Swietenia macrophylla) on Udyan Path.
Tree has been chopped and mutilated to accommodate for the electric installations.

Here is another great example of the total lack of coordinated planning from every angle – the road, pedestrian traffic, electric installation and tree plantation etc.

6.6 Photograph of a high speed, double carriage road in Panchkula, is an example of the pedestrian path provided adjoining the road. There is no assigned space for trees which have been planted far away from the road.

The following are all the things that are principally wrong:

1. There is no assigned space for the tree.

2. Small structured flowering trees have been planted far away from the road curb which are totally out of scale and non functional.

3. The pedestrian path is adjacent to the road.

4. The electric lines are right next to the pedestrian path and installed along the line of trees leading to interference with tree plantation.

5. The trees have been chopped and mutilated to accommodate for electric installations.

All the energy and time in growing the trees is wasted due to all above stated factors. The impact of this kind of approach is evident as there is no visual appeal, no shade, hence no value in planting trees along the road side.

Tree plantation in Delhi, planned and executed by Lutyens over a century ago is an example of ideal application of fundamental concepts of roadside tree plantation.

6.7 Photograph shows the planned tree plantation done by Lutyens.

The photograph above shows a view of a road where:

1. Plantation has been done on the road verge creating a visual green tunnel

2. Large structured trees have been used providing a complete cover on the road and on the pedestrian paths

3. Electric installations have been planned and laid underground. They do not interfere with the trees.

4. Pedestrian paths are set away from vehicular traffic.

Ideal road cross-sections

Trees take a very long time to develop their personality and become fully functional. For this reason tree plantation has to be incorporated into the initial design and planning of city roads. The reason this is not widely done is because of financial constraints. Limited resources make development of roads and electric installations a priority neglecting tree plantation. Appropriate space has to be assigned for trees right from the start. Things cannot be altered after the trees have attained maturity. To plan for increased traffic needs in the future additional space should be provided in the central verge of the road. This will allow for road widening towards the central verge rather than the sides and hence avoid any mutilation or removal of trees that take a long time to grow.

About Chandigarh roads it is added that the base of Chandigarh city plan is rectangular grid of heavy traffic roads enclosing the self-contained sectors. The fast moving traffic is restricted to the rectangular grid of heavy and fast traffic roads which are designated V2 and V3. These roads are at the outer sides of the sectors. Inside the sectors, protected fast traffic, are the V4, V5 and V6 roads which provide access to shopping centres, schools, hospitals as well as houses etc.

1. The access roads to houses are called V6 roads. These are either 30 or 40 feet wide.

2. The shopping street roads are known as V4 roads. These are mostly 120 feet wide but some of these are 160 feet wide too.

3. The major circulation roads within the sectors are designated as V5 roads. These are either 60 feet or 80 feet wide.

4. The fast moving traffic roads around the sectors separating each sector are called V3 roads. These are mostly 100 feet wide but some of these roads are also 120 feet in width.

5. The main approach roads to the city which too are heavy traffic and fast speed roads are called V2 roads. These

roads are 160 feet or even up to 200 feet width.

6. Almost the same pattern of road system exists in Mohali as well as Panchkula.

Shown here are standard road cross sections indicating the ideal space for plantation of trees. Detailed cross sectional illustrations of road spacing of 30 feet, 40 feet, 60 feet, 80 feet, 100 feet, 120 feet, 160 feet and 200 feet give clear specifications for metalled portion of the road itself, the central verge, space for tree plantation, pedestrian paths, slow carriage ways as well as space for installation of over head electric lines.

These standard specifications will be effective, functional and can be applied to all roads anywhere in the country.

Small roads of 30 feet and 40 feet width, typically approach roads to homes require only one row of large structured, tall trunk trees with spreading crown. These roads because they are narrow, only need one row of trees of a single kind. They will help create an excellent green cover, visually appealing to residents. Overhead electric power lines and street lights are planned on the opposite side of the road. Another consideration for small roads is the orientation of the sun. Vertical roads running north - south trees should be planted on the eastern side of the road. The horizontal roads running east - west plantation should be done on the southern side of the road. This is especially important on small roads that have only a single row of trees on one side of the road.

Perfect road cross-sections of all kinds of roads stated above are presented here in the form of diagrams.

Ideal road cross-sections - Illustrated:

6.8 An ideal design of plantation of 30 feet wide access roads to homes running in north-south direction. Trees are planted on the eastern side of the road.

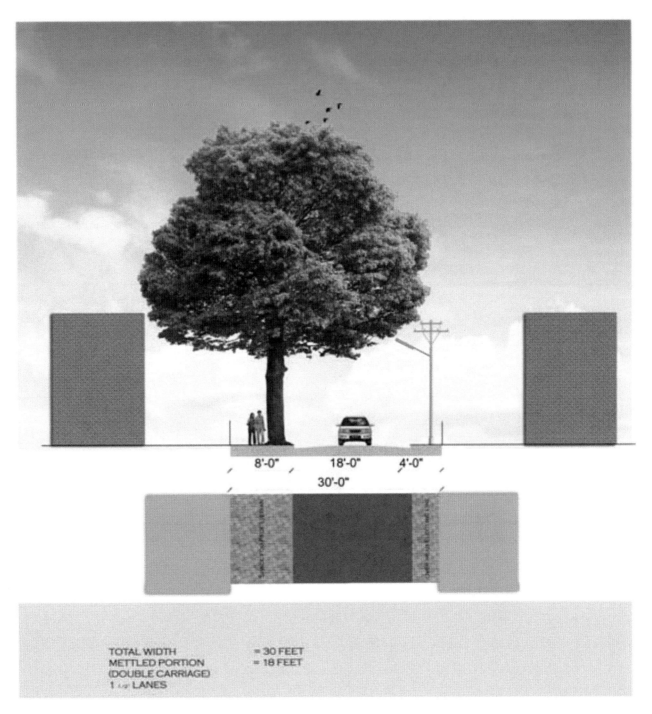

6.9 An ideal design of plantation of 30 feet wide access roads to homes running in east-west direction. Trees are planted on the southern side of the road.

6.10 An ideal design of plantation of 40 feet wide access roads to homes running in north-south direction. Trees are planted on the eastern side of the road.

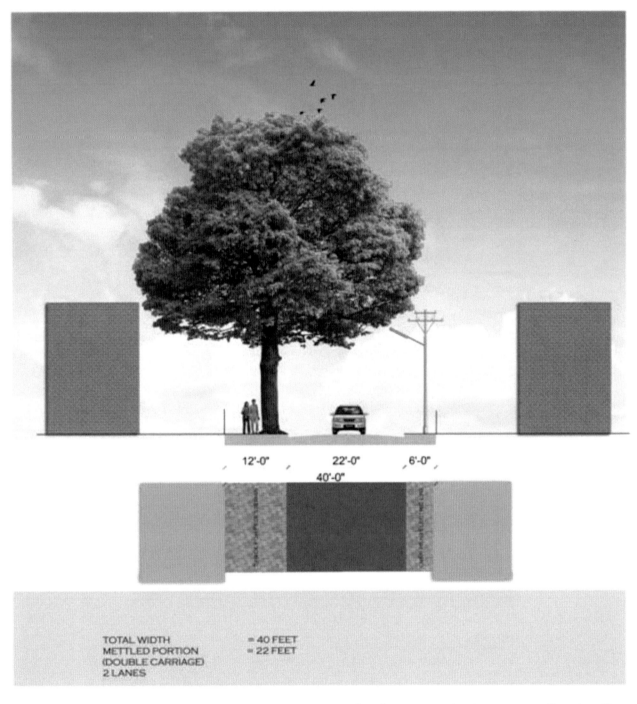

6.11 A perfect design of plantation of 40 feet wide access roads to homes running in east-west direction. Trees are planted on the southern side of the road.

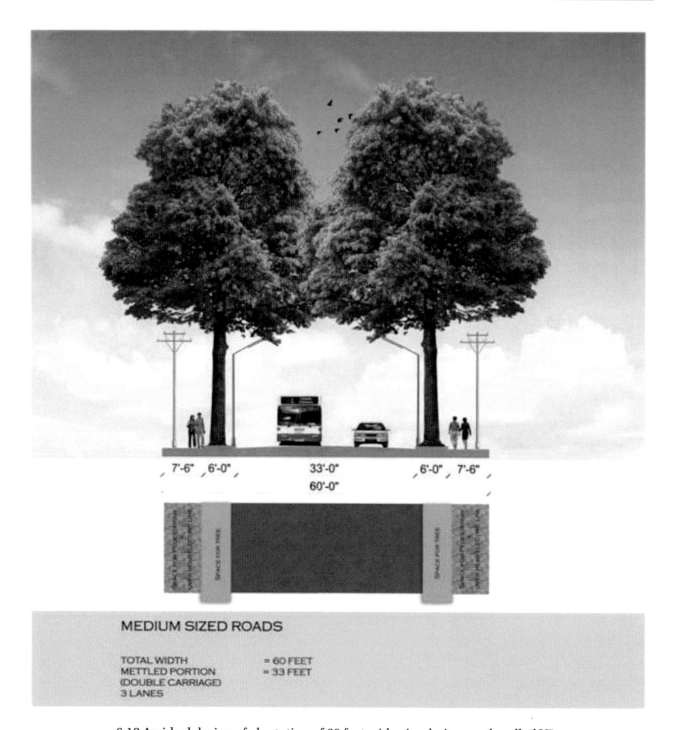

6.12 An ideal design of plantation of 60 feet wide circulation roads called V5.

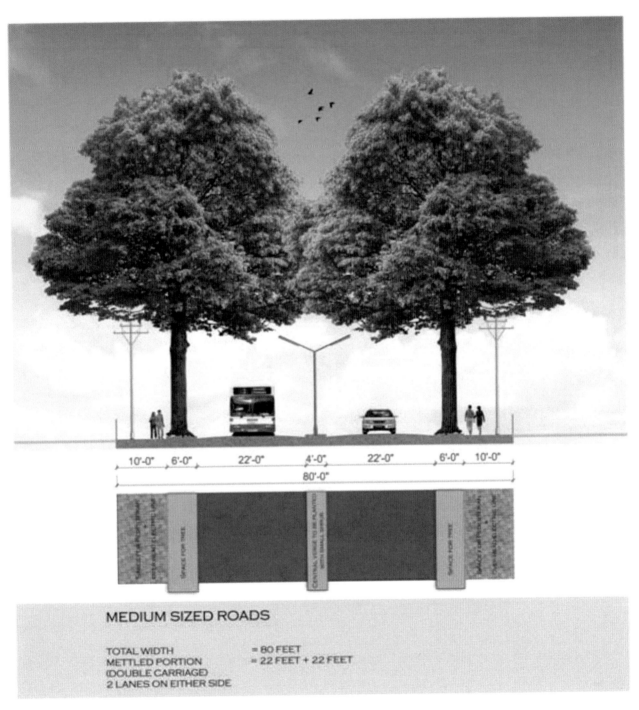

6.13 An ideal design of plantation of 80 feet wide circulation roads called V5.

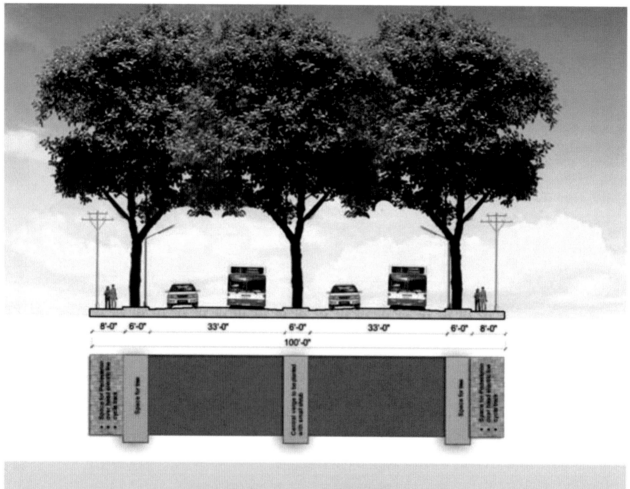

Total Width = 100 Feet
Mettled Portion = 33 Feet + 33 Feet
(double carriage)
3 Lanes on either side

6.14 A perfect design of plantation of heavy and fast moving traffic roads around sectors called V3 roads.

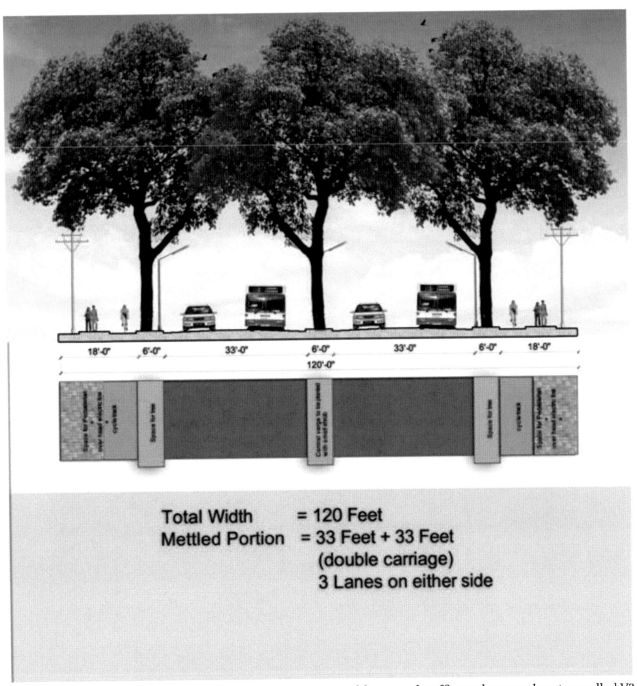

6.15 An ideal design of plantation of 120 feet wide heavy and fast speed traffic roads around sectors called V3 as well as shopping streets of the same width known as V4.

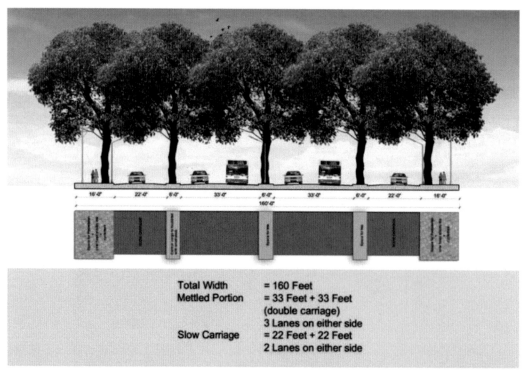

Total Width = 160 Feet
Mettled Portion = 33 Feet + 33 Feet
(double carriage)
3 Lanes on either side
Slow Carriage = 22 Feet + 22 Feet
2 Lanes on either side

6.16 An ideal design of plantation of 160 feet wide shopping streets within the sectors called V4 as well as heavy traffic and fast speed approach roads to the city called V2.

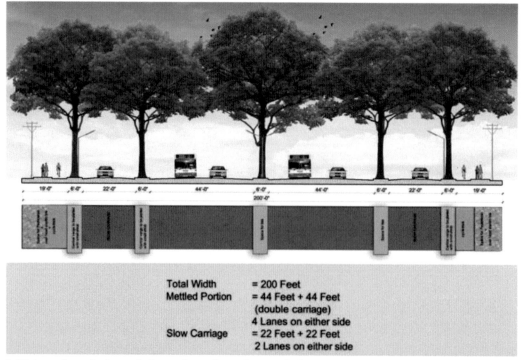

Total Width = 200 Feet
Mettled Portion = 44 Feet + 44 Feet
(double carriage)
4 Lanes on either side
Slow Carriage = 22 Feet + 22 Feet
2 Lanes on either side

6.17 A perfect design of plantation of 200 feet wide heavy traffic and fast speed approach roads to the city called V2.

TREE PLANTING PLANS FOR BUILDINGS

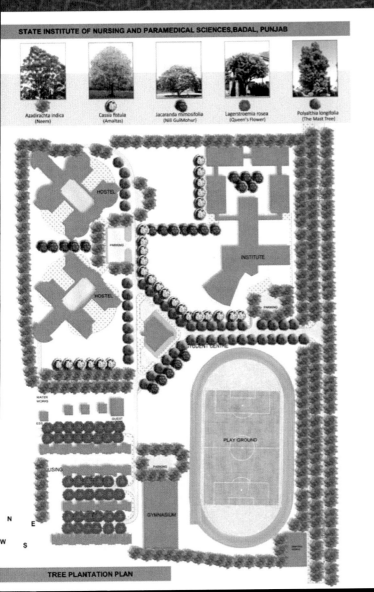

STATE INSTITUTE OF NURSING AND PARAMEDICAL SCIENCES, BADAL, PUNJAB

Azadirachta indica (Neem)
Cassia fistula (Amaltas)
Jacaranda mimosifolia (Nili GulMohur)
Lagerstroemia rosea (Queen's Flower)
Polyalthia longifolia (The Mast Tree)

HOSTEL

PARKING

HOSTEL

INSTITUTE

PARKING

STUDENT CENTRE

WATER WORKS

GUEST

HOUSING

PLAY GROUND

PARKING

GYMNASIUM

TREE PLANTATION PLAN

TREE PLANTATION PLAN GOVERNMENT COLLEGE SARDULGARH, PUNJAB
DETAILS OF TREES

Swietenia macrophylla (Mahogani)
Polyalthia longifolia (The Mast Tree)
Acacia auriculiformis (Australian kikar)
Jacaranda mimosifolia (Nili Gulmohar)
Cassia fistula (Amaltas)

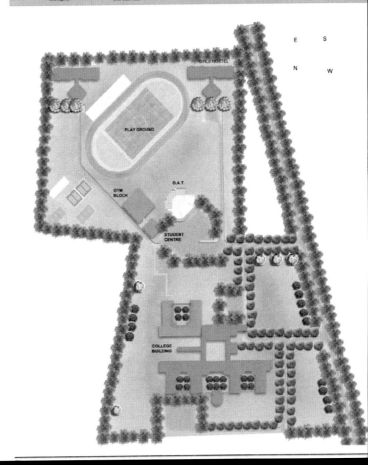

GIRLS HOSTEL

PLAY GROUND

GYM BLOCK

O.A.T.

STUDENT CENTRE

COLLEGE BUILDING

URBAN habitat comprises of both, public and private buildings that include offices, universities, colleges, hospitals, factories, community centres, museums, and other large or small civil or civic buildings. These areas also need professionally and aesthetically planned landscaping by way of tree plantation. Trees are a permanent inscription on a site and therefore have to be planted very carefully. Most trees have a long life and once established they continue to perform the desired function of serving mankind for several decades. Moreover, growing trees is a cheap, low maintenance and very effective method of bringing about qualitative improvement of buildings. Raising trees around buildings is much easier than growing them on roads and open spaces in the town. Trees planted within building premises are not exposed to toxins from automobile exhaust etc. They are also relatively more protected from physical abuse by human beings as well as stray cattle. Being in protected space around buildings, they develop perfect sizes, shapes and colours.

Trees add life and soul to a building. Trees are graceful and grand and when planted in a planned manner enhance the beauty of buildings. Tall and majestic trees on approach roads of buildings, around boundary walls and on vistas leading up to the buildings lend distinct character to a building complex. Trees also help in creating spaces within the buildings and help break the rigid lines of the building facade giving it an attractive, natural look.

Trees are also a source of shelter. They can be any size and shape, planted in any arrangement, rows or groups; they help keep structures cool in summer and warm in winter. Apart from sheltering, greening and improving environment of buildings, trees help create a micro climate reducing air-pollution, air temperature, dust, noise and most of all better the health, efficiency and productivity of humans.

Fundamental Principles of Planting Around Buildings

The fundamental principles and concepts adopted for tree plantation plans around the buildings are the same as those for plantation around roads, open spaces and parks in the city.

Spacing of trees is one of the most important measures. Although trees can grow at any spacing planting them right distance apart will add to their effective growth. When they are planted too far apart they grow numerous side branches on the trunk and develop low crowns. This keeps them from growing to the right height and meeting appropriate scale requirements. Trees planted closely together develop tall, straight trunks and high, narrow crowns. This allows them to come together to make a splendid, high canopy of branches and foliage.

Another important concept is the use of a single species of trees on a particular site. That helps bring coherence from similarity of structure, texture and pattern. It helps create an excellent collective impact. Mixing up too many kinds creates visual disorder and looks unattractive.

The placement of trees is another important aspect of tree plantation around buildings. Unplanned, random plantations create disorder and reflect a profound misunderstanding of nature. Trees are natural and any way they are planted be it in straight rows or geometric patterns, they look natural and interesting. Therefore carefully planned plantation can add beauty to a building complex.

It is necessary to thoroughly integrate buildings and sites in terms of space, form, material and function. The views of the building from outside and inside should be perfect. Trees should add scale and complement the architectural mass of a building. Only a few species should be used to create structures for shade, shelter and green covers. Flowering trees should be used to aesthetically enhance the building and to make the entire building space colourful and attractive.

The following section discusses well laid out plans of building campuses where all these principles have been applied. It highlights that spaces around buildings should be developed in a manner that provides a distinctive personality and a unique physical environment of a building.

The plantation plans explained here show the size of the buildings, their scale and orientation. The plans demonstrate the trees used for shade and greening along approach roads, on the vistas leading to the buildings, and around various spaces of the buildings. Details about the kind of species to be used, the spacing, the training of trunks and development of crowns has been explained. Trees on approach roads and vistas have been planted close to the verges so that the crowns of the tree unite and provide a complete green cover on the roads after attaining the desired height of the trunk

The plantation plans explaining details of each plan in respect of the following buildings are presented in this chapter.

1. Dr. Vidya Sagar Institute of Mental Health, Amritsar, Punjab.

2. State Institute of Nursing and Paramedical Sciences, Badal, Punjab.

3. Agriculture Bhawan, Mohali, Punjab.

4. Multi-Purpose Sports Stadium, Jalalabad, Punjab.

5. Hockey Stadium, Rajindra College, Bathinda, Punjab.

6. Government College, Munak, Punjab.

7. Government College, Sardulgarh, Punjab.

8. Government College, Chunni Kalan, Punjab.

9. Seed Farm, Shero Bagha, Amritsar, Punjab.

10. Centre of Excellence for vegetables, Kartarpur, Punjab.

11. Centre of Excellence for fruits, Hoshiarpur, Punjab.

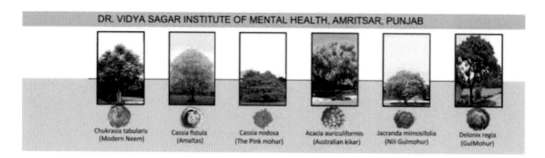

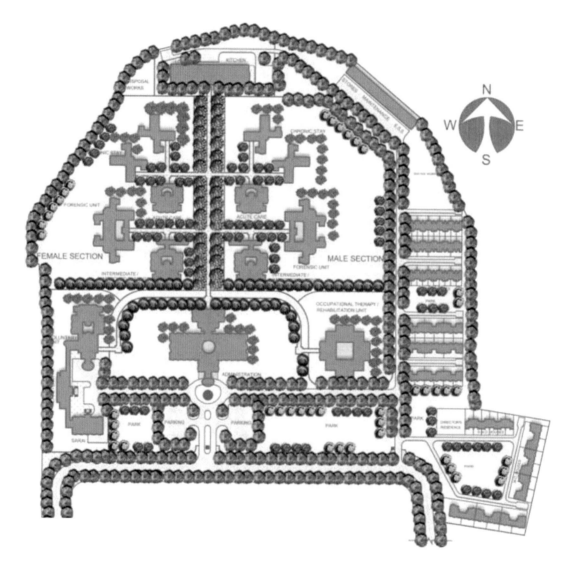

7.11 Tree Plantation Plan

Dr. Vidya Sagar Institute of Mental Health, Amritsar, Punjab

Landscapist: H.S. Johl
Architect: Sarbjit Bahga
Area: 47.40 Acres

Details of trees used for plantation:

1. Chukrasia tabularis (Modern Neem)
2. Cassia fistula (Amaltas)
3. Cassia nodosa (The Pink Mohur)
4. Acaic auriculiformis (Australian Kikar)
5. Jacaranda mimosifolia (Nili Gul Mohur)
6. Delonix regia (Gul Mohur)

Concept:

Chukrasia tabularis is a beautiful, evergreen tall, stately tree. It creates tall, majestic green walls and enhances the beauty of the Institute. This tree has been planned for plantation around the approach road and internal roads, parking area, around the entire boundary of the campus, spaces separating administrative block, patient areas, the laundry area and the kitchen. It will create green, high tunnels on approach roads and roads leading to the administrative block, the cafeteria, sarai and road separating residential areas and going upto the kitchen block. It will screen off the undesirable haphazard growth outside this campus and will help create an excellent livable environment inside the campus. This tree provides shelter, creating air conditioning, helps reduce dust and noise. All of this is beneficial for the health of patients and staff. Repeated use of this single kind of tree will look good and will fill up the spaces in a short amount of time. Using a single kind of tree will also help in unifying spaces and will produce an impressive collective impact with its uniform structure, texture of branches and foliage.

Massive plantation of flowering trees consisting of Amaltas, Nili Gul Mohur, Pink Mohur, Gul Mohur and Australian Kikar in large groups of each will brighten up the entire campus with colour and beauty. These trees bear very pretty flowers and create a mass effect of bright crimson, yellow, blue and pink flowers.

Planting hints:

1. All the trees be planted at a spacing of 15 feet (centre to centre).

2. The trunks of all chukrasia trees planted on approach roads, internal roads and parking area be trained upto the height of 20 feet. By doing this the roads will develop green cover on the entire space and the extensive view of the building will be visible. The parking area will get plenty of sunlight in winter months and will keep the areas warm.

3. The trunks of Chukrasia trees planted around the periphery as well as all kinds of flowering trees be raised to the height of 10 feet and thereafter crowns be allowed to develop. This will enable the boundary area to have the needed green belt of trees. It will also help develop attractive shapes of flowering trees leading to a brilliant colour effect. With close planting the branches of the trees will intermingle and a continuous canopy of branches, foliage and colour will develop in a very short period of time.

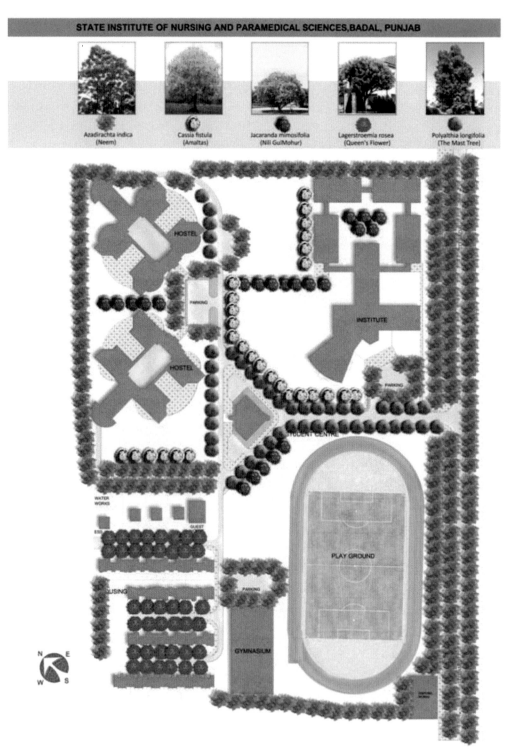

7.2 Tree Plantation Plan

State Institute of Nursing and Paramedical Sciences, Badal, Punjab

Landscapist: H.S. Johl
Architect: Sarbjit Bahga
Area: 22.62 Acres

Details of trees used for plantation:

Azadirachta indica (Neem) Polyalthia longifolia (The Mast tree) Lagerstroemia rosea (Queen's flower) Cassia fistula (Amaltas) Jacaranda mimosifolia (Nili Gul Mohur)

Concept:

Neem tree has been planted on the approach road, boundary of the entire campus, around parking areas and hostel buildings. It is a unique large structured evergreen tree that helps create a distinct personality of the campus. Repeated use of this single kind of tree at close spacing creates healthy tall green walls. It helps create homogeneous structure, texture and pattern and produces excellent collective impact. The branches of the tree intermingle and create a continuous network which looks splendid. With close planting tall straight trunks with narrow crowns develop in a short period. The green walls will screen off the haphazard growth on the outside and will create a unique physical environment within the premises, providing shade, shelter, attractive spaces and breaking the rigid lines of the building facade.

Polyalthia longifolia develops tall straight trunk and excellent narrow crown. Its plantation on approach road and roads

leading to hostel blocks and road around canteen creates beautiful vistas leading to the campus.

The queen's flowers, Amaltas and Nili Gul Mohur have been planted in groups and rows. These will add grandeur, colour and beauty to the entire building complex, residential areas and hostel blocks.

Planting hints:

1. All the trees be planted at spacing of 15 feet (center to center) in rows and groups as shown in the plan.

2. The plantation of roadside trees be done on verges.

3. Trunks of the Neem trees around approach road and parking area be trained as a single stem upto the height of 20 feet. By doing this parking area will get lot of winter sun and approach road will develop as a nice green tunnel and view of the building will become clearly visible.

4. The trunks of the Neem tree around the boundary of the campus be trained up to 10 feet height. By doing this the green walls will be created at low height to screen off any undesirable views.

5. The trunks of all the flowering trees be trained upto a height of 10 feet and then allowed to develop crowns.

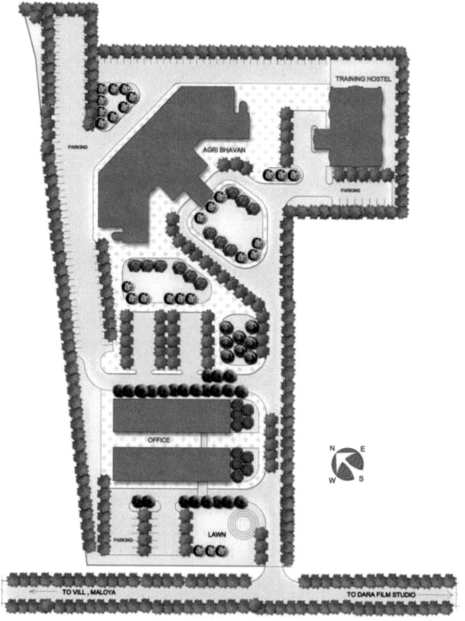

7.3 Tree Plantation Plan

Agriculture Bhawan, Mohali, Punjab

Landscapist: H.S. Johl
Architect: Sarbjit Bahga
Area: 5.76 Acres

Details of trees used for plantation:

1. Swetenia macrophylla (Mahagony)

2. Polyalthia longifolia (The Mast tree)

3. Cassia fistula (Amaltas)

4. Jacaranda mimosaefolia (Nili Gul Mohur)

5. Delonix regia (Gul Mohur)

6. Lagerstroemia rosea (Queen's flower)

Concept:

Mahagony provides total green cover on the approach road, creates tall stately boundaries of the campus, provides shade in parking areas in summer and when trained to have a 20 foot high trunk provides sufficient winter sun and brightens up the area. The trunks of trees around a boundary are trained upto 10 feet height to obtain screening and creating better views. A congenial, comfortable, noiseless exclusive physical environment will develop and screen any unplanned, haphazard growth outside the campus.

Repeated use of a single kind of trees at close spacing will look fantastic and will fill up spaces in a short amount of time. It will also help unify spaces and produce an impressive collective impact of the same kind of structure, texture and spacing.

The Mast tree on narrow roads within the campus will meet the scale requirement and create vistas of distinct character.

Amaltas, Jacaranda, Gul Mohur and Queen's flower are beautiful flowering trees that profusely produce yellow, blue, red and deep pink flowers, respectively. These are arranged in rows and groups and will create a magnificent floral display when they are in bloom.

Planting hints:

1. All the species of trees be planted at close spacing of 15 feet (centre to centre).

2. Trees around approach road and within the campus be planted close to the road curb.

3. The trunks of the trees on the approach road and parking areas be trained as a single stem up to the height of 20 feet and then allowed to develop crowns.

4. The trunks of the trees around the boundary of the campus and those of all the flowering trees are trained upto a height of 10 feet and then develop crowns.

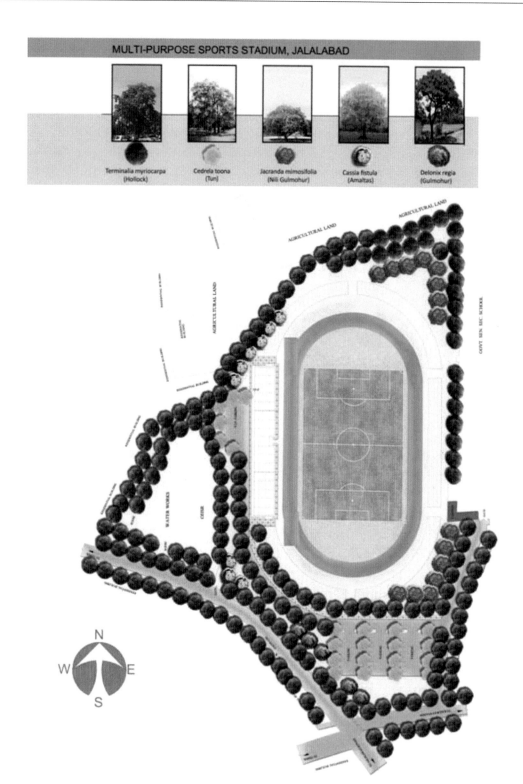

7.4 Tree Plantation Plan

Multi-Purpose Sports Stadium, Jalalabad, Punjab

Landscapist: H.S. Johl
Architect: Sarbjit Bahga
Area: 11.15 Acres

Details of trees used for plantation:

1. Terminalia myriocarpa (Hollock)

2. Cedrela toona (Tun)

3. Cassia fistula (Amaltas)

4. Jacaranda mimosifolia (Nili Gulmohur)

5. Delonix regia (Gul Mohur)

Concept:

Hollock is one of the most attractive and functional trees It possesses outstanding qualities because of which it is considered as ideal for tree plantation around building campuses. Hollock is evergreen, develops a straight tall trunk and excellent crown. Its crown looks beautiful in autumn months when the tree is profusely blooming bearing brilliant deep pink flowers. It is a very neat tree and does not spread litter. Hollock has been used for planting on the main approach road going to Jalalabad bypass, approach road to the stadium as well as the entire boundary of the campus. Repeated use of this tree looks fantastic, helps in unifying spaces and produces a very good collective impact on account of the uniform structure, texture of branches and foliage as well as spacing.

The Hollock tree will provide a green enclosure effect and create a unique environment for the entire campus and around roads. It will provide an excellent tall green roof.

Tun is a deciduous tree. It sheds foliage in winter and will therefore allow sunlight in the parking areas keeping them bright and warm in the cold season. During summer its foliage offers a green cover and provides shade.

Amaltas, Nili Gul Mohur and Gul Mohur are very beautiful flowering trees. These are arranged in large groups and will make the entire sports stadium look colourful when they are in full bloom.

Planting hints:

1. All the trees are planted at a spacing of 15 feet (centre to centre).

2. The plantation of roadside trees is done on verges.

3. Trunks of the trees around the campus are raised to 10 feet height and then crowns are developed.

4. Trunks of roadside and parking area spaces are raised to 20 feet height till crowns develop.

5. Trunks of all the flowering trees are raised to 10 feet height and then crowns developed.

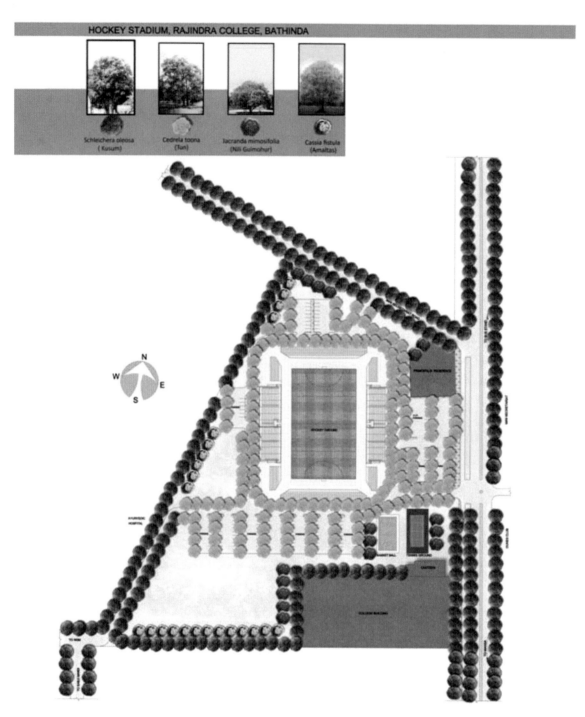

7.5 Tree Plantation Plan

Hockey Stadium, Rajindra College, Bathinda, Punjab

Landscapist: H.S. Johl
Architect: Sarbjit Bahga
Area: 17.39 Acres

Details of trees used for plantation:

1. Schleichera oleosa (kusum)

2. Cedrela toona (Tun)

3. Jacaranda mimosifolia (Nili Gulmohur)

4. Cassia fistula (Amaltas)

Concept:

kusum is a very attractive tree. It is structurally big, very hardy, and durable and is suitable for planting around roads and the boundary of building campuses. The foliage of the tree is very colourful. It sheds old leaves for a short period in early summer, produces sparkling scarlet coloured new leaves in spring season which turn dark green in summer and rainy season and then become brilliant yellow in autumn.

Using only this one tree for plantation on the approach roads and the entire boundary of the Hockey Stadium campus will produce excellent collective impact. The uniform structure and texture of tree branches and the foliage combined with an arrangement of uniform spacing will create a great visual environment for the entire campus. It will bind spaces creating an impressive mass impact. The tree will build tall, green and colourful walls around the boundary of the campus and a grand, tall cover of green, yellow and red colours on the approach road.

Tun is a very functional tree. It has been used for plantation around the narrow roads of the hockey stadium and around parking areas. This tree provides excellent green cover on the roads in summer months and sheds leaves in winter thus keeping the entire spaces warm and bright.

Amaltas and Nili Gulmohur are beautiful flowering trees. They bloom profusely and make the entire campus colourful and attractive. Their plantation has been arranged in large groups to obtain mass effect of colour.

Planting Hints:

1. All the trees are planted at a spacing of 15 feet (centre to centre).

2. Roadside trees are planted on road verges.

3. Trunks of trees around campus are raised to 10 feet height and then crowns developed.

4. Trunks of roadside trees of kusum and Tun as well as around parking area are developed to 20 feet height before crowns are developed.

5. Trunks of flowering trees be raised to 10 feet height and then crowns developed.

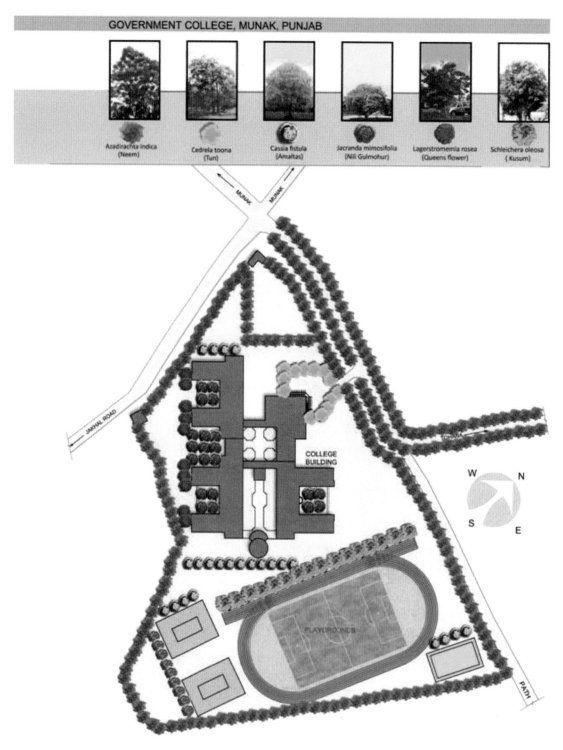

7.6 Tree Plantation Plan

Government College, Munak, Punjab

Landscapist: H.S. Johl
Architect: Department of Architecture, Punjab.
Area: 10.71 Acres

Details of trees used for plantation:

1. Azadirachta indica (Neem)

2. Cedrela toona (Tun)

3. Cassia fistula (Amaltas)

4. Jacaranda mimosifolia (Nili Gulmohur)

5. Lagerstroemia rosea (Queen's flower)

6. Schleichera oleosa (kusum)

Concept:

Neem is an outstanding tree with very good qualities which makes it ideal for plantation around building campuses for shade and beauty. It is used on the approach road and boundary of the entire campus.

Repetitive use of Neem on the approach road and around the boundary lends personality to the campus. Planting close to the verges of roads, growing straight, tall trunks and narrow, high crowns provide a complete green cover on the road and will make the approach very attractive. The trunks of the trees around the road are raised to 20 feet height so that the extensive views of the project and buildings are not blocked.

Around the boundary of the campus, a wide, tall green wall develops which screens off the unpleasant growth outside college campus. Also it creates an excellent green enclosure, creating pleasant environment within the campus. The trunk of trees around the campus should be trained to only 10 feet height and then crowns with a continuous higher canopy of branches and foliage allowed to develop.

Cedrela toona sheds leaves in winter and therefore is appropriate for parking spaces. It will allow a lot of sun which keeps the areas warm and bright in winter and shade in summer.

Schleichera oleosa (kusum) is another excellent large structured tree. Its foliage is colourful which adds brilliant yellow, red and green colours in various seasons. This tree provides shade and separates the space of the play area.

Amaltas, Nili Gulmohur, Queen's flower are outstanding flowering trees. These have been arranged in rows and groups making the entire campus colourful.

Planting hints:

1. All trees are to be planted at a spacing of 15 feet centre to centre.

2. Trees around roads are to be planted close to the verges.

3. The trunks of tree on the approach road are to be trained as single stem up to 20 feet height.

4. The trunks of trees on the boundary are to be trained to 10 feet height and then crowns developed.

5. The trunks of flowering trees to be raised to 10 feet height and thereafter crowns are developed.

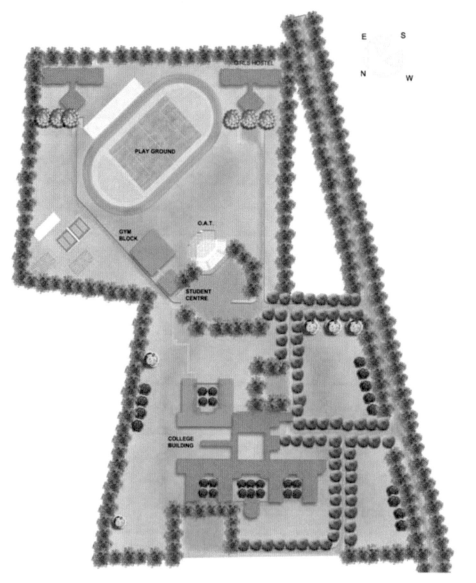

7.7 Tree Plantation Plan

Government College, Sardulgarh, Punjab

Landscapist: H.S. Johl
Architect: Department of Architecture, Punjab.
Area: 19.73 Acres

Details of trees used for plantation:

1. Swietenia macrophylla (Mahagony)

2. Polyalthia longifolia (The Mast tree)

3. Acacia auriculiformis (Australian Kikar)

4. Jacaranda mimosifolia (Nili Gul Mohur)

5. Cassia fistula (Amaltas)

Concept:

Mahagony has been planned on the approach road and along the entire boundary of the campus including the parking area. Massive use of only this single outstanding tree makes the medical college rich in structure, texture and distinctly different. The close dense plantation adds grandeur to all the spaces. The trees help in greening, air conditioning and improving the air quality of the building campus.

The tall straight trunk with narrow crown of the Mahagony tree around the campus creates impressive and effective green walls. Its plantation around approach roads provides a green cover on the entire road. This tree also creates spaces, separating the college building from residential areas.

Polyalthia longifolia, the Mast tree, is an evergreen tree that creates tall stately vistas leading to the main building. It develops a greenwalkways with a high arching roof of branches and foliage, that helps in sheltering and creating a background for setting rows of flowering trees.

Flowering trees are aesthetically arranged around the college building as well as open spaces in rows and groups. Amaltas, Nili Gulmohur and Australia Kikar create a magnificent floral display when they are in bloom. Large scale plantation of these flowering species will make the entire campus colourful.

Planting Hints:

1. All trees are planted 15 feet apart (centre to centre).

2. Plantation of trees around approach road, internal roads, parking areas be done on verges.

3. All trees along the boundary have their tree trunks trained as a single stem upto the height of 10 feet and then crowns developed. Same be done with all the flowering trees within the campus.

4. Trunks of trees around approach roads and parking areas are trained as single stem upto 20 feet height and then crowns developed. This will allow transparency and a visual grasp of the building and the approach very impressive. Parking areas will get plenty of sun in winter and shade in summer.

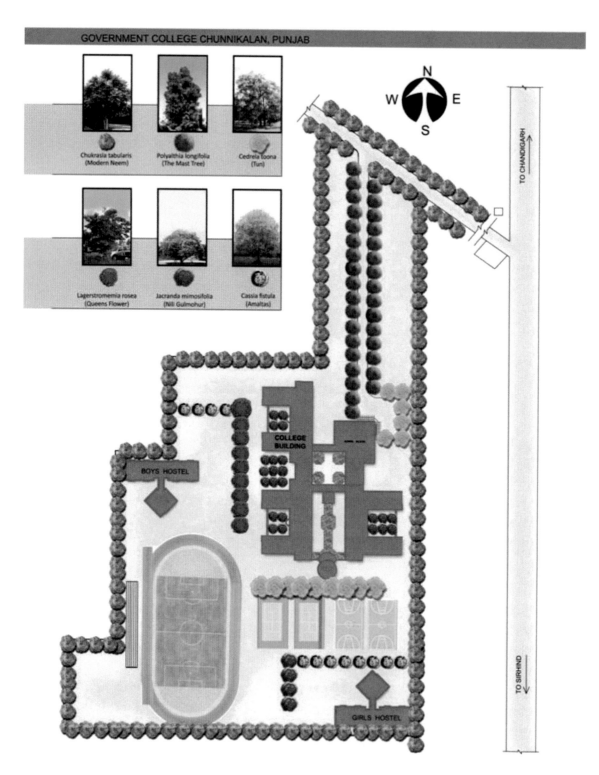

7.8 Tree Plantation Plan

Government College, Chunni Kalan, Punjab

Landscapist: H.S. Johl
Architect: Department of Architecture, Punjab.
Area: 14.11 Acres

Details of trees used for plantation:

1. Chukrasia tabularis (Modern Neem)

2. Polyalthia longifolia (The Mast tree)

3. Cedrela toona (Tun)

4. Lagerstroemia rosea (Queen's flower)

5. Jacaranda mimosifolia (Nili Gul Mohur)

6. Cassia fistula (Amaltas)

Concept:

Chukrasia is a beautiful and functional tree for plantation around buildings. It is evergreen, fairly fast growing and performs the function of developing a tall, effective green belt around the building campus. It helps create excellent green cover on the approach roads of the campus.

Chukrasia will develop high trunks, a narrow crown, arching roof of branches and foliage around the road providing a green cover on the entire approach road. This tree provides greenery, creates a micro climate, reduces dust and noise and improves the overall environment.

Polyalthia longifolia planted around the narrow approach road to the college building develops tall evergreen stately and majestic vistas leading to the main building.

The Tun tree is used in the parking lots. It sheds leaves in winter months keeping the parking space sunny and warm. In summer months its foliage provides excellent shade.

Queen's flower, Nili Gulmohur and Amaltas bloom profusely producing bright pink, mauve and yellow flowers, respectively. All these trees are planted in large numbers in rows and groups to make the entire campus colourful.

Planting hints:

1. All trees be planted at 15 feet close spacing (center to centre).

2. Tree plantation around roads is done close to the verges.

3. Trunks of trees around in parking area and approach road are trained as single stem upto the height of 20 feet.

4. The trunks of trees around the campus and those of flowering trees within the campus be trained as single stem to 10 feet before crowns are formed. Flowering trees at a low height puts up a better display of flowers.

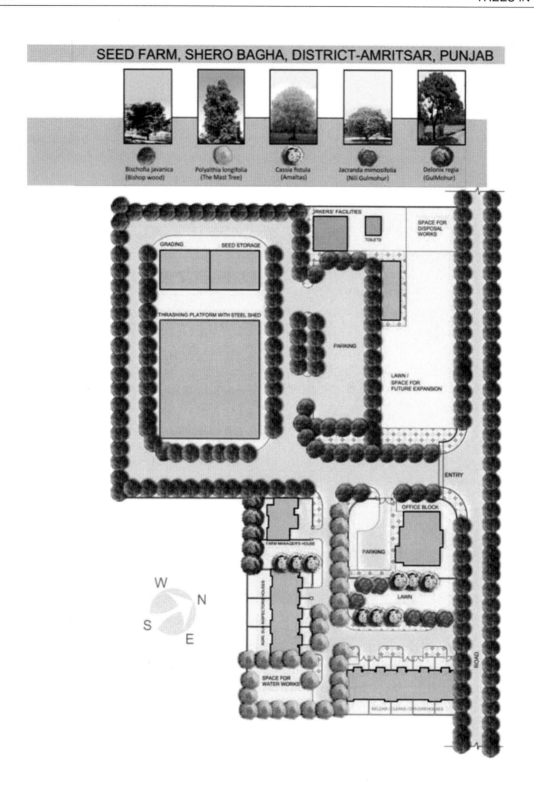

7.9 Tree Plantation Plan

Seed Farm, Shero Bagha, Amritsar, Punjab

Landscapist: H.S. Johl
Architect: Sarbjit Bahga
Area: 3.55 Acres

Details of trees used for plantation:

1. Bischofia javanica (Bisho wood)

2. Polyalthia longifolia (The Mast tree)

3. Cassia fistula (Amaltas)

4. Jacaranda mimosifolia (Nili Gul Mohur)

5. Delonix regia (Gul Mohur)

Concept:

Bischofia javanica is a very pretty tree with superior qualities that makes it very suitable for plantation around building campuses. It is a neat, evergreen tree that does not spread litter. Bischofia is planted all over, along the outer approach road, on the inside approach road of the campus, around the boundary of the working area and also in the parking area. It provides shade, screens undesirable views outside the complex, creates a tall, stately green wall and helps improve the micro climate creating better work conditions.

The trunks of the trees around the boundary are trained to a height of 10 feet, but the trunks of trees on the approach roads and parking area are trained upto 20 feet height. This arrangement provides a complete green cover of branches and foliage on the road and brightens up the area with letting in bright light in winter and summer sun. Winter sun helps keeps the parking area warm and bright. Close plantation helps in developing tall straight trunks and effective crowns in short periods and keeps from trees developing dense, low-branched crowns. Using this single kind of tree helps form a continuous, arched canopy that produces visual unity.

Plantation of the Mast tree on narrow roads spearates work and living spaces and meets the scale of the area.

Amaltas with its brilliant yellow flowers, Nilli Gul Mohur with bright blue flowers and Gul Mohur with its crimson blooms will add a lot of colour and beauty to the campus. They all bear flowers profusely and look glorious planted in rows or in clusters.

Planting hints:

1. All kinds of trees are planted at a spacing of 15 feet (centre to centre).

2. Trees on outer approach road as well as those inside the campus be planted close to the curb.

3. The trunks of the trees on outer approach road, approach roads to the campus as well as parking areas be trained straight upto the height of 20 feet and then crowns developed.

4. The trunks of flowering trees are trained as single stem upto the height of 10 feet and then crowns are developed.

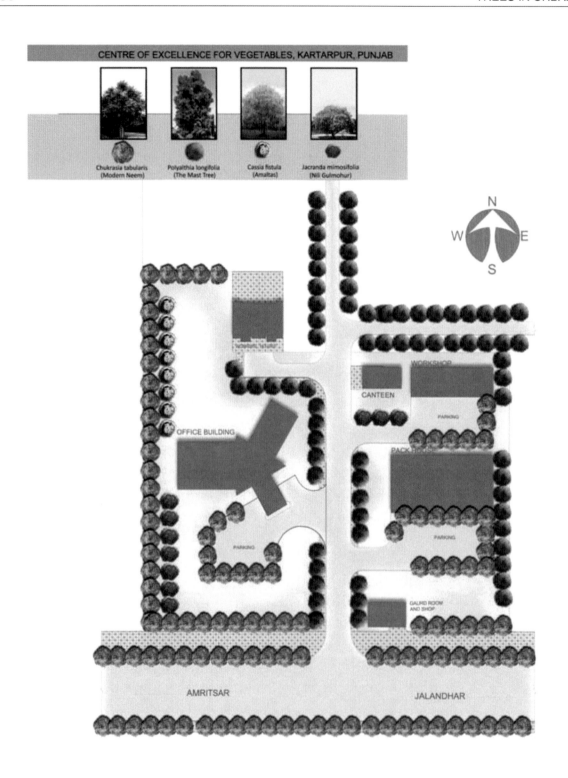

7.10 Tree Plantation Plan

Centre of Excellence for Vegetables, Kartarpur, Punjab

Landscapist: H.S. Johl
Architect: Sarbjit Bahga
Area: 2.02 Acres

Details of trees used for plantation:

1. Chukrasia tabularis (Modern Neem)

2. Polyalthia longifolia (The Mast tree)

3. Cassia fistula (Amaltas)

4. Jacaranda mimosifolia (Nili Gul Mohur)

Concept:

Chukrasia is one of the most attractive evergreen trees, with dark green foliage. It is fairly fast growing and has all the good qualities that make it one of the best trees for planting around and within a building campus for shade and beauty.

Chukrasia has been planted around main highways i.e. Jalandhar-Amritsar road. It is also planted around the boundary wall and parking lot of this complex. The trunks of the tree on the main highway are raised upto 20 feet height to give the entire road the needed green cover. That same approach is applied in the parking lots within this campus. This allows the winter sun to permeate through providing warmth and brightness. Around the boundary, the trunks of the trees are trained upto 10 feet height to create a screen and provide shelter..

The Mast trees are tall, and majestic. When planted on approach roads they develop grand vistas separating the office building from the working space. The space on the eastern and northern side of the boundary wall is narrow. This tree will develop tall, evergreen structure performing all the required functions of greening, developing natural screening from undesirable outside views and providing shelter to the entire campus.

Amaltas and Jacaranda have been planted in the open spaces around the office and the canteen building. Both these flowering trees bloom profusely and produce brilliant yellow and mauve flowers respectively. These trees add a lot of colour and beauty to the campus when they are in full bloom.

Planting hints:

1. Plantation of all kinds of trees be done at close spacing of 15 feet (centre to centre).

2. The plantation of trees on the outer approach road and within the building roads and parking areas be done close to the verges.

3. The trunks of the trees on the main approach road as well as parking areas be trained as single stem upto the height of 20 feet and then crowns developed.

4. The trunks of the trees on the boundary wall as well as all the flowering trees are trained as single stem upto the height of 10 feet and thereafter crowns developed.

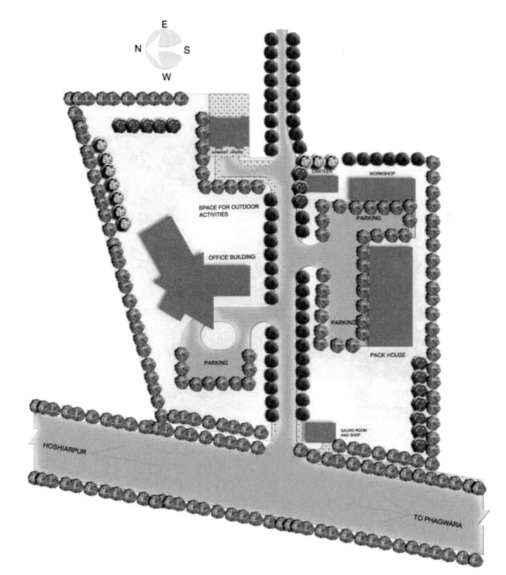

7.11 Tree Plantation Plan

Centre of Excellence for Fruits, Hoshiarpur, Punjab

Landscapist: H.S. Johl
Architect: Sarbjit Bahga
Area: 2.92 Acres

Details of trees used for plantation:

1. Chukrasia tabulasis (Modern Neem)

2. Polyalthia longifolia (The Mast tree)

3. Cassia fistula (Amaltas)

4. Jacaranda mimosifolia (Nili Gul Mohur)

Concept:

Chukrasia tabularis, an evergreen tree has been planned around approach roads and around the boundary as well as in parking areas. This tree provides shade and a green cover to all the approach roads. It builds tall, stately walls around the campus that provide shelter and improve the micro climate of the total space around the building.

Chukrasia on approach roads and parking areas is grown straight to the height of 20 feet before its crown develop. This arrangement provides the entire road a cover of branches and foliage and parking areas gets sufficient winter sun to brighten up the entire space.

The Mast tree around approach road creates stately vistas and provides a green cover separating office and residential buildings from the work spaces.

Amaltas and Nili Gul Mohur are beautiful flowering trees. Their setting around office open space, canteen and working area will provide massive colour and will liven the campus when these trees are in bloom.

Planting hints:

1. Plantation of all kinds of trees be done at close spacing of 15 feet (centre to centre).

2. The plantation of trees on the outer approach road and within the building roads and parking areas be done close to the verges.

3. The trunks of the trees on the main approach road as well as parking areas be trained as single stem upto the height of 20 feet and thereafter crown of the trees developed.

4. The trunks of the trees on the boundary wall as well as all the flowering trees are trained as single stem upto a height of 10 feet and then crowns developed.

8

ENTIRE CITY PLANNED AS A PARK - A CONCEPT

URBAN residents require an escape from the everyday hectic life. People from cities want to go to the countryside, to some attractive spots closer to nature for relaxation and peace of mind and even for recreation. At the bottom of every person's heart is a yearning for the primordial forest, for nature. Parks in and around cities are created and developed to serve this need.

The idea of parks is more than 22 centuries old. The Chinese evolved natural gardens in the second century B.C. The concept of parks was introduced in Japan in sixth century A.D. Both these countries have developed world class natural gardens. They are pioneers in the creation of romantic, picturesque gardens and creating spaces using plant material artistically in a very specialized way.

The concept of creating recreational gardens also developed in Central and South Asia, India and western countries in the seventeenth century. Formal gardens based on regular, geometric straight lines were developed in Egypt, Rome, renaissance Italy, Turkey, France, England and Mughal India. These were gardens mostly based on rational planning. Architectural elements such as buildings and stairs along with water were the main features of these gardens. Plants played a minor role and were generally laid out in formal lines and beds.

Everywhere in the world gardens were and are created as an imitation of nature to satisfy the instinct of every human being to find an escape from the hustle and bustle of town life. The need for seeking solace in undisturbed natural environment of pastoral areas and forests etc. may not arise, if the entire city can be developed as a park and the beauty and serenity of nature can be recreated in the city.

Trees are the only elements that can do wonders in developing the entire city as one green mass that can take the shape of a park. This concept can be realized if all the spaces in the city are planted abundantly, extensively and continuously with trees in an aesthetic manner.

A highly planned city like Chandigarh can take the shape of a park if the entire urban environment that includes roads, buildings, open spaces, parks and all places of living, working, and recreation, shopping and playing are planted with trees in a planned manner. Human artistry can achieve this objective and if Chandigarh can succeed in doing this it can be a model for the entire country.

In this chapter the concept of developing an entire city as a park is demonstrated by using Chandigarh's sector 28 as an example. The key successes in planning and design as well as the weaknesses in execution are highlighted in this chapter. An entire city can be created applying this concept broadly and at a large scale.

Also the possibilities for obtaining perfection in the task pertaining to various roads and parks have been discussed and presented.

Nature in the form of trees should flow like air in every possible space in a city. There should be no bare spots that are devoid of these fascinating, beautiful and natural materials available to mankind. Trees bind all the spaces in the city together bringing about unification and cohesiveness in the entire landscape of the city.

Planting only one kind of tree species in a single area of the city helps in unifying

8.1 Sector dividing V3 road in Mohali Continuous row of Chukrassia trees without any break look aesthetically beautiful and help in realizing the concept of developing city as a park.

8.2 Circulation road in Sector-17 Repetitive use of closely planted large structured Sterculia trees present an excellent composition.

8.3 Circulation road in Sector 36 Single kind of large structured Terminalia bellirica (Bahera) trees helps in unifying the spaces creating a distinct collective impact.

the individual parts into a single whole. The repetitive use of closely planted large structured kinds produces an excellent composition because of the homogeneity in structure, texture of branches and foliage.

All the spaces consisting of streets, squares and parks can be linked together by an intricate ceiling of tree branches. In contrast to scattered use of trees, their collective use in groves, rows and symmetrical units used in groupings and various kinds of settings help in unifying the spaces resulting in developing the city as one big park and creating a distinctly superior collective impact.

The V3 - sector dividing road of Sector 28

Sector 28 of Chandigarh is surrounded by Purv Marg on the east, Chandi Path on the west, Madhya Marg on the north and and Udyog Path on the west. All these sector dividing roads known as V3 roads are very well planted.

Purv Marg has a very wide green belt dividing the residential areas of the city from the Industrial area. It is planted with 8 rows of mango trees on either side. This has helped build a massive green area in the city. The problem however is that the trunks of the trees on this road have not been trained.

The low growing trees block the extensive views of the city. Ideally the trunks of the trees should be raised to at least 20 feet and then crowns are developed. Doing this will greatly improve the look of the road.

8.4 Photograph showing extensive plantation of mango trees on Purv Marg. Even the central verge has been planted with mango trees.

Chandi Path is exclusively planted with Terminalia arjuna (Arjan) trees. A photograph of the pure avenue of Arjan on this road looks excellent.

8.5 **Chandi Path on the western side of sector 28, Chandigarh** - Continuous rows of Terminalia arjuna (Arjan) trees without any gap has helped develop the V3 road around this sector very well

Plantation on Madhya Marg is also functionally satisfactory. Although this road has a mix of many species used that adversely affects the aesthetic setting of the road, the plantation is functional because the trees have been planted in continuity.

8.6 **Tree plantation on Madhya Marg on the northern side of sector 28** - A mixture of many species is planted on this road. But because there is continuity in plantation the desired effect is achieved.

Udyog Path is one of the very well planted avenues in Chandigarh. This road is the biggest contributor to the attractive greening of Sector 28. It is planted with Swietenia macrophylla (Mahagony) tree that has attractive structure, texture and foliage.

8.7 **Udyog Path on the west side of sector 28, Chandigarh** - Swietenia macrophylla (Mahagony) creates a magnificent avenue.

The V4 - shopping street of Sector 28

The V4 in sector 28 is planted with many different kind of tree species. The trees are also planted far away from the road curb. As a result the parking spots in this area are bare and treeless. The photographs of these areas illustrate how there is no continuity in tree plantation due to which there is no greening effect. Ideally, a single species of trees should be planted around the road and in the parking spaces.

8.8 **Shopping street sector 28, Chandigarh** - The parking area is bare and treeless. The continuity of green cover is missing thus defeating the purpose of creating city as park.

8.9 **Shopping street sector 28, Chandigarh** - The wide parking space without trees looks bare and dull. It should be entirely covered with a green cover of trees, creating the effect of a park.

8.10 **Car park area** - The treeless space looks monotonous and drab.

In contrast to these streets of sector 28, the shopping area in Mohali has an attractive green cover that provides shade, comfort and natural beauty. A similar pattern of tree plantation would be ideal in the shopping parking area of sector 28, Chandigarh.

8.11 Parking area on shopping street, sector-63, Mohali.

The plan below shows the right way to plant this street and the adjoining parking area. This will provide an excellent green cover, bring about unity, cohesiveness and a grand roof of branches and foliage in the entire shopping space, hence achieving the concept of developing the entire area as a park

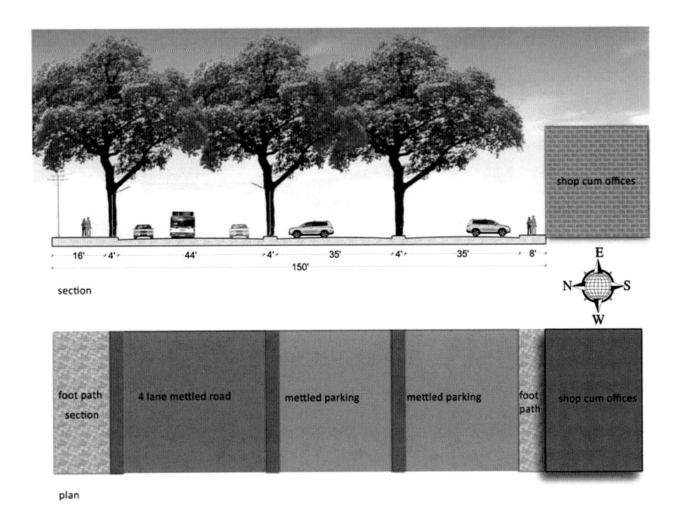

V4 road sector 28 chandigarh
Total width of road =150 feet wide
Lanes = 4 no's
Parking on south side = 74 feet wide

8.12 Diagram shows the ideal method of planting the V4 road with excellent single kind of tree species. Trees have tall straight trunks and upright high branched crowns

The V5 - circulation road of sector 28

The V5 is one of the most important roads of a sector. Circulation roads are broad in size and can be planted with one row of trees on either side. Large structured trees will provide a green cover on the entire road for the vehicular traffic as well as for pedestrians. The use of one kind of tree will unite the spaces on and around this road and help achieve the effect of city as a park.

The sector photographs of this road running through sector 28 a, b, c and d show how this important circulation road is bare and quite treeless. Whatever planting exists is not planned. A diverse mix of trees is used, some planted by home owners of houses adjoining the main roads.

8.13 **Circulation road, sector 28a, Chandigarh (Western side)** - Plantation is minimal and haphazard.

8.14 **Circulalation road, sector 28a, Chandigarh (Northern side)** - The road is without any trees. There are numerous gaps and many kinds of species used in variable sizes and shapes. Poorly installed electric lines are running on either side of the road. All of these features account for not letting the city be developed as a park.

8.15 **Circulation road, sector 28b, Chandigarh (Eastern side)** - There is no continous green cover, electric installations are visually unattractive. Lack of planning defeats the purpose of greening the city and developing it as a park

8.16 **Circulation road, sector 28c, Chandigarh (Eastern side)** - There are several kinds of trees that don't really serve any purpose Electric lines have been installed right next to the row of trees. There is no continuous park like effect.

8.17 **Circulation road, sector 28d, Chandigarh (Western side)** - The road is treeless with nothing to help break the concrete jungle like unnatural effect. This is contrary to the park like effect that is very desirable for comfortable city living.

8.18 **Circulation road (V5), sector 28c, Chandigarh** - The entire road is without any tree. Whatever plantation is visible, it is within the boundary walls of the various public buildings on this road. Electric lines are also badly installed.

The following defects are glaringly obvious from the photographs of this road.
1.Trees are planted haphazardly, not serving the purpose of providing green cover on the street.
2.Several gaps and unplanted spaces have broken the continuity of greenery
3. A mixture of many species varying in size and shape have been planted

4. Small structured flowering trees that do not meet the scale requirements have been planted in some spots
5. Trees have not been planted uniformly at the appropriate space from the road and from each other
6. Electric installation have are not planned in conjunction with tree plantation

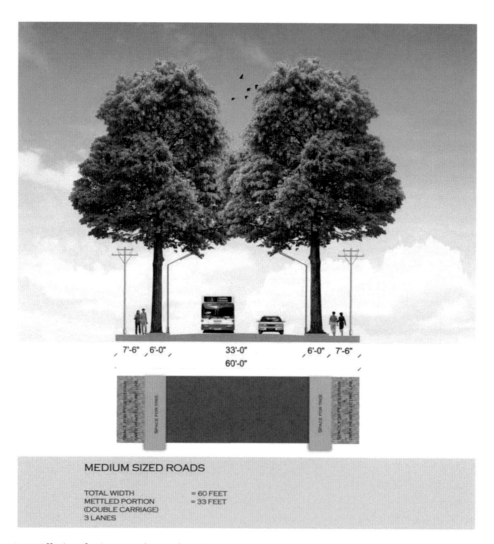

8.19 All circulation roads in Chandigarh are either 60 feet or 80 feet wide. Ideal tree plantation includes a double row of trees of the same kind of species. The correct way of installing electric poles in relation to trees is also shown in this diagram. Tall straight trunked and high branched crown trees should be used.

All these reasons account for the inability in developing the entire city as a park. Tree plantation, if done right and in a planned manner can help create a city as a park. The landscape plan below shows the correct way to plant the V5 circulation road of sector 28. It also shows how the appropriate spacing of trees and power lines as well as vehicular and pedestrian traffic.

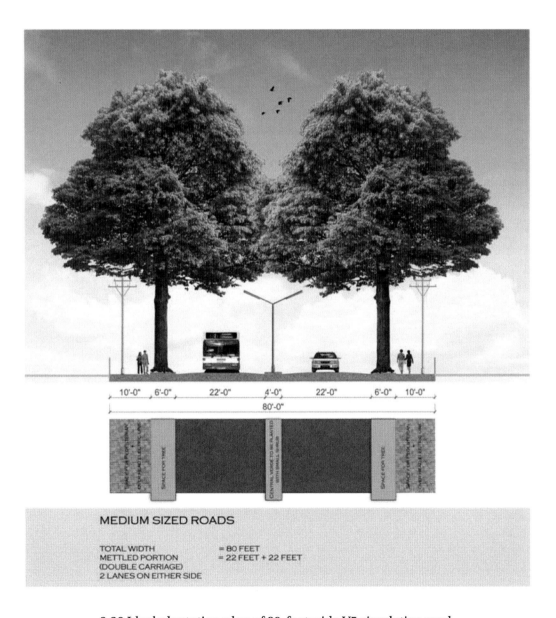

8.20 Ideal plantation plan of 80-feet wide V5 circulation road.

The V6 - access roads to dwellings in sector 28

The V6 is a narrow road that can be planted with one row of trees. The power lines can be installed on the opposite side of the road from where the trees are planted so they do not conflict with each other. Tree crowns will develop unrestricted and can spread and provide green cover on the entire space of the road thus bringing nature right up to the living space.

The photographs, below of many V6 roads in sector 28 show that almost all the roads are treeless and look drab. Thus, the entire sector including the living spaces, roads and shopping areas that constitute the major portion of the sector are without any trees and look lifeless.

8.21 **Access road to dwellings, sector-28a, Chandigarh** - Most of the road is without any tree and without the necessaary green cover. Electric power lines are installed in a haphazard manner.

8.22 **Access road to dwellings, sector-28b, Chandigarh** - This approach road to houses is without any green cover. Electric power lines are in the the space where trees should be planted.

8.23 **Access road to dwellings, sector-28c, Chandigarh** - A treeless residential area and park.

8.24 Access road to dwellings, sector-28d, Chandigarh - The entire approach road to the residential area is quite bare of trees. Whatever few trees are visible are planted in a haphazard manner by the homeowners.

8.25 Access road to dwellings, sector-28d, Chandigarh - The entire long stretch of the road is without an adequate tree cover. Electric lines are not installed in a planned manner.

Apart from Sector 28, below are photographs of some of the roads in other sectors with similar problems. Shopping street roads known as V4, sector circulation roads called V5 and access roads to dwellings called V6 roads in sectors 8, 15, 37, 44 are planted in almost the same way as those in sector 28. Tree plantation has not been done on most of the V4, V5 and V6 roads in the city.

8.26 Photograph of the shopping street V4 in Sector 44 shows the entire area without any tree cover.

8.27 Circulalation road (V5), Sector 8, Chandigarh The road does not have a continuous row of trees. The pedestrian passasge is constructed right next to the main road.

8.28 **Approach road to dwellings (V6) sector 15 d, Chandigarh** - Absolutely treeless road. Ideally a wide green cover can be created.

8.30 **Approach road to dwellings (V6) sector 44, Chandigarh** - Entire residential street without trees.

8.29 **Approach road to dwellings (V6) sector 37 c, Chandigarh** - Living spaces looking drab without any trees. Electric power lines are installed without any planning.

For locations highlighted above some ideal plantation plans and road sections are presented below. It would be appropriate to use single kind of trees in each street to create a homogenous composition. There will be uniformity of structure, texture of tree branches and its foliage. This approach will provide comfort, beauty and nature in every living space in the city.

8.31 Diagram shows horizontal road running from east to west. Trees on these roads are planted on southern side of the road.

TOTAL WIDTH   = 30 FEET
METTLED PORTION   = 18 FEET
(DOUBLE CARRIAGE)
1 ʜᴏʀ LANES

8.32 Diagram shows vertical road running from north to south. Trees on these roads are planted on eastern side of the road.

Parks of Sector 28

City parks are mostly developed as gathering grounds of various kinds of activities rather than as places to experience nature. Parks can be developed with natural forms from beautiful trees, shrubs and numerous kinds of plants. However, as the photographs below illustrate the parks in sector 28, as in other sectors are not developed thoughtfully. They demonstrate cluttered haphazard plantation.

8.33 **Children Park, sector 28a, Chandigarh** - Most of the area in the park is without flowering trees, shrubs and attractive plants.

8.34 **Park in sector 28a, Chandigarh**- This is a huge park area. It is one large bare green patch of grass, without trees, shrubs and flowers.

8.35 **Park in sector 28c, Chandigarh** - The entire space of the park is empty and bare. It is large space that can ideally be developed as an interesting landscape garden. A little glimpse of a V6 road on the right side of the park is also without trees.

8.36 **Park in sector 28c, Chandigarh** - The entire space of the park is without any tree, shrub or any kind of plant. Photograph shows absolute clutter and total neglect of the space in the residential area.

8.37 Flowering trees are small in structure and meet the scale requirements of the spaces of the gardens. Thus they are suitable for planting in parks and should be used extensively in large groups to create massive effects of colour.

Flowering Trees in Parks

Trees play a significant role in developing parks in urban areas as special kind of gardens. Parks constitute as one of the important areas of an urban habitat. These are spaces where nature can be displayed in the form of trees, shrubs, attractive plants including stones and water. A city park with these elemental components would fulfill create a setting of inspiring simplicity.

Flowering kinds of trees are small in structure and meet the scale requirements of smaller spaces typical of city parks and gardens. Such trees are suitable for planting in parks and should be used extensively in large groups to create attractive spaces with massive colour effect. Flowering trees should be planted in a planned manner, close to each other. This will allow their branches to intermingle and develop, green and colourful walls that can be trained to vary from 12- 18 feet in height and 8-16 feet in width. Repeated use of flowering trees in curvy spaces and planned informal settings result in interesting spaces in a park.

To convey the conceptual design for arranging and setting flowering trees appropriately three parks of large, medium and small size are prepared here. The salient features of these parks along with their conceptual plans are given below.

Large sized park

The total area of this park is about 15 acres. Four big spaces each comprising two portions measuring an area of about 3.5 acres have been created. The park has got one entry from each side of the road and two entries to each space within the park. Three kinds of flowering trees are planted i.e. Jacaranda mimosifolia (Nili Gulmohar), Cassia fistula (Amaltas), Delonix regia (Gulmohar) that profusely bloom and produce shining mauve, brilliant yellow and scarlet flowers, respectively.

Apart from flowering trees, beautiful green trees have been planned around and within the park. This forms an interesting background and setting for the flowering trees and also gives an identity to the park. Abundant use of flowering trees will make each space glorious. Adding numerous kinds of shrubs, roses, herbaceous borders and the prized ornamental kinds of flowering plants will enhance the beauty of these spaces. Informal footpaths will bring about suspense and make the walk in the garden interesting. The beauties and subtleties of each space will be unfolded gradually and not thrust all of a sudden

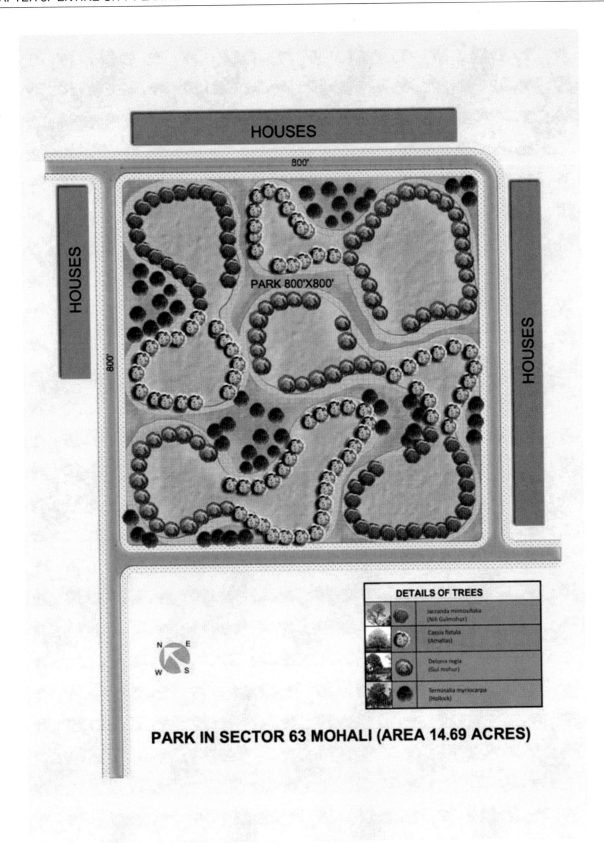

8.38 Schematic plan of large sized park.

Medium sized park

This park has been planned in 10 acres of area. It is split into five big spaces repeatedly using one of three kinds of flowering trees. Each space has been planted with one kind of flowering trees. Jacaranda mimosifolia (Nili Gulmohar), Cassia fistula (Amaltas) and Delonix regia (Gulmohar) which profusely bloom are planted in each space. The flowering trees are planted in very large groups. They are planted closely so that their branches intermingle with each other and create beautiful spaces that will spread in a fairly wide space and attain a proportionate height. For a medium sized park only one entry to the park is planned from the road side and two entries to each space within the park.

One outstanding kind of green structured tree has been planted to give a special character to this park. Informal spaces will look aesthetic and make the walk interesting with unique views at every spot unfolding natural beauty while walking on the foot path into each space. The big spaces measuring an area of about 2 acres each with flowering trees will enable the setting of all kinds of beautiful shrubberies and various kinds of perennial as well as annual species of plants.

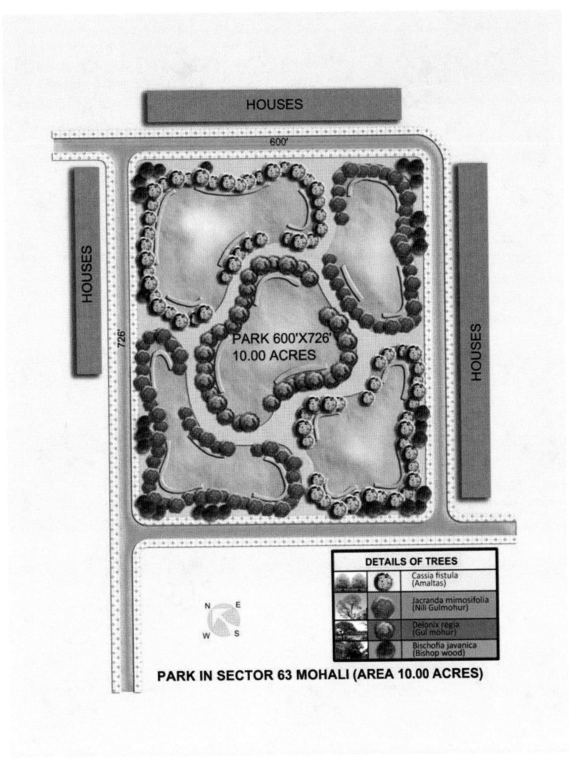

8.39 Schematic plan of medium sized park.

Small sized park

The small park has been planned in an area of almost five acres. It has three big spaces; each a little over 1.5 acres in size. Lagerstroemia rosea (Queen's flower), bearing massive pink and mauve flowers and Bauhinia variegata (Kachnar) also bearing brilliant red, pink and mauve flowers have been planned in each space. The third space has been planted with Cassia nodosa (The Pink Mohar). The plantation of flowering trees has been done in a thoughtfully, planned manner at very close spaces so that their structures, branches and foliage develop interesting wide and tall walls that get loaded with massive flowers creating spectacular areas. A single kind of green tree has been planned around the park to create a background for the flowering trees and give specific character to the park. Three entries, one from each side of the road have been provided. Each space within the park has two passages. Footpaths for walking in the park have been planned in a regular manner which will make the walk interesting and attractive. Like big and medium parks, attractive shrubberies and miscellaneous kinds of plants varying in height and spread of about six feet can be planned within each space that has an area of more than one acre.

Additionally, every park big or small in size should be developed as an uncluttered space, dominated by a reticulum of trees growing through the mantle of wonderful natural materials displayed in an artistic manner. We should use only trees, shrubs, attractive plants for the city parks and all else should be superfluous.

The story of all other city sectors in Chandigarh is similar to that of Sector 28.

The existing condition of almost all the open spaces, parks, public and private buildings as well as areas around roads within the sectors is the same as that discussed in sector 28. Most of the streets are without any green cover and whatever little plantation is visible is the result of a casual approach, lacking any planning. An enormous amount of effort is needed to set things right and achieve success in creating cities as parks.

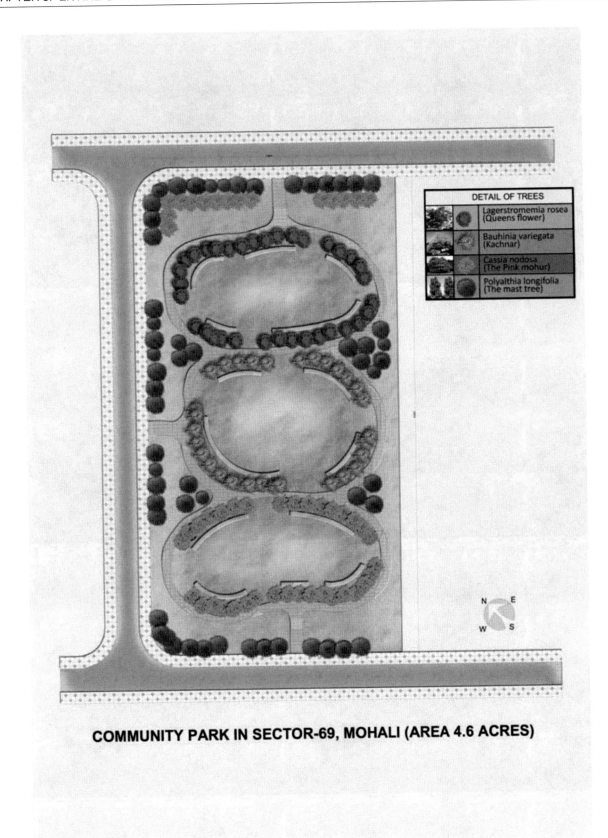

COMMUNITY PARK IN SECTOR-69, MOHALI (AREA 4.6 ACRES)

8.40 Schematic plan of a small sized park.

9

TREES FOR CITY ROADS

THIS chapter emphasizes on the salient features of various kinds of trees suitable for plantation around urban roads. A detailed description of select trees accompanied with photographs highlights the structure and patterns of branches and foliage of a selection of trees.

As discussed earlier, tree structure is the most important consideration in selecting and using trees on city roads. Trees described in this chapter have excellent structure and are therefore suitable and desirable for roadside plantations.

The large structure of these trees makes them suitable for use to produce excellent design and perform the following important functions:

- Develop straight tall trunks. The superior texture of their branches, foliage and spreading crowns makes them very attractive. These trees create natural walls, ceilings and enclosed room like spaces that create a great environment

- Provide the required green cover on the entire space between buildings and roads

- Enhance urban elements and broaden the architectural views of the city.

- Modulate space vertically and develop an excellent ceiling of branches and foliage with transparency, height and create a uniform pattern of light and shade on the street.

- Provide aesthetic beauty. Their plantation at narrow spaces binds the entire city together

- They are strong, sturdy and durable and stand abuse from environmental pollution.

- These large structured trees are suitable for the agro-climatic conditions of the local north-Indian region and require little care and maintenance.

- They are healthy if grown close enough for their branches to intermingle and create a strong network of the crown due to which these trees also get strength.

- Trees with large structures naturally have a deep root system due to which there is no danger of their getting uprooted or broken by wind storms or any other environmental hazards.

- The deep roots also prevent them from causing damage to underground services such as sewers, storm water, electric and drinking water lines.

Terminalia myriocarpa (Hollock)

Terminalia myriocarpa (Hollock) is an outstanding tree with superior qualities that make it an ideal tree for plantation in the urban habitat. Of all the species of Terminalias, this particular one is the most attractive and very functional. It is a large structured tree that can attain a height of over 60 feet and a crown spread of more than 40 feet. The tree develops a straight, tall trunk, forms an excellent crown and provides cover on the entire space between buildings and roads. The entire crown looks attractive in autumn months when it flowers as pendent boughs loaded with light yellow blooms which turn to bright pink.

It is a neat, evergreen tree that doesn't shed leaves and does not spread any litter. The tree is very hardy, and pollution tolerant. Due to all of these qualities, this tree is highly recommended for extensive use for plantation around city roads as well as buildings and parks .

It can be grown in tropical, sub-tropical and sub-montane regions that have good arrangements for irrigation. Young saplings require heavy and frequent irrigations. This tree has excellent growth in well drained rich loam, sandy loam and clay loam soils.

Ficus microcarpa (Indian Laurel Tree)

Of all the different kinds of Ficus species, this one is undoubtedly the most outstanding and most elegant. The Laurel tree has a lot of the qualities that make it an excellent large structured tree for plantation around wide city roads.

Its grey coloured trunk is very strong and can be developed to any desirable height. The tree makes an interesting, massive crown with a lovely mixture of long vertical, rounded and drooping branches. New shining leaves grow all year around. They are light rose to chartreuse in colour which gives the tree a pleasing two tone effect throughout the year.

This tree is a native of India and Malaysia. It is very sturdy, and is ideal for big avenues and road side plantations in urban areas. It can grow in a wide range of climatic and soil conditions. All areas up to an elevation of 4000 ft. above mean sea level and all kinds of well drained clay, loam, rocky and stony soils are suitable for its growth.

Azadirachta indica (Neem)

Azadirachta indica (Neem) which is called the Pride of India truly has the qualities that make it ideal for plantation around city roads. It has been used extensively on New Delhi roads. Neem is a large structured tree, very suitable for wide city roads. It develops a tall, strong trunk and an extensive large spreading crown. The tree trunk can be raised to any desired height of over 60 feet and a crown that spreads more than 40 feet. Neem is an attractive, functional tree that remains evergreen throughout the year except in early summer when it sheds leaves for a short period of time. It is very hardy, sturdy and durable. Neem is resilient to the effects of pollution. It is also resistant to termites. Neem tree has a lot of other uses. It has medicinal properties that make it an essential ingredient for mosquito repellants. Its seeds and foliage are used to make organic manure. Other parts of the tree are used for manufacturing organic pesticides as well as valuable organic food for plants. Neem trees grows wonderfully well in tropical, sub-tropical, arid, sub-montane and sub-temperate zones. They do well in a wide range of soil conditions including sandy, loamy, clayey, stony and even alkaline.

Schleichera oleosa (Kusum)

Kusum is a strikingly pretty tree that is structurally very big and strong. The trunk of the tree can be raised to a considerable height. It develops an excellent spread out crown and is highly suitable for plantation around wide city roads.

It is a deciduous tree dropping its entire old foliage in early summer months for a short period. Soon thereafter the tree produces a wealth of glorious new shiny colourful leaves. The entire tree sparkles with vivid splashes of crimson foliage that turn light green and then dark green as they mature. In autumn months too, the foliage changes colour to brilliant yellow. So, in essence the tree continuously changes colours of red, green, and yellow all the year lending beauty to the landscape. Its beauty makes it a perfect tree for extensive use for aesthetic plantations, landscaping and beautification of cities.

It is very hardy and sturdy. It is able to withstand extreme environmental pollution and helps reduce the effects of air toxins from automobiles as well as urban and industrial habitats. The tree grows in tropical, sub-tropical climate at upto 3000 feet above sea level and is also good for sub-mountain and sub-temperate zones. It needs well drained sandy loam, gravelly loam and clay loam soils. It does not grow in saline soils with poor drainage. Tree has a tendency of branching at low height so it needs to be trained for best results.

Chukrasia tabuaris (Modern Neem)

Chukrasia is a beautiful, very functional tree suitable for plantation around wide city roads. The tree is structurally large, evergreen, fast growing, hardy, durable, and pollution resistant. It has dark green foliage, and is excellent for creating avenues. The tree has a strong trunk and massive crown. Its trunk can be developed to any desired height. Its large crown provides excellent green cover over more than 40 feet wide roads. Chukrasia is a neat tree that does not spread litter.

This tree grows very well in tropical, sub-tropical and even arid regions and wide range of well drained loam, sandy loam and clay-loam soils.

Swietenia macrophylla (Mahagony)

Mahagony is one of the finest trees for landscaping and beautification. The tree has a large structure that makes it very suitable for plantation around wide roads in urban areas.

It is evergreen and fast growing. It has dense dark green attractive foliage that helps create an avenue. The Mahagony tree is hardy, durable and pollution resistant. The trunk of the tree can be developed to any desired height and because of its massive crown, it serves the purpose of providing a green cover on the entire space between the roads and buildings in the urban street. It is a neat tree and does not litter.

Mahagony is ideal for extensive greening in cities. It grows well in tropical, sub-tropical, sub-mountain and even arid regions and performs very well in sandy loam, loam and clay loan soils that have plenty of organic matter. The tree needs good drainage for good growth.

Kigelia pinnata (Sausage tree)

It is a large tree, with a thick trunk and spreading crown. Most of the time during the year it is green. Kigelia is a very functional tree for urban plantation that is hardy, durable and fast growing tree with good foliage. The trunk of the tree can be developed to a big height and because of its massive crown and pollution resistant qualities it is suitable for plantation around big highways. It is an exotic tree originally from tropical Africa but grows exceedingly well in the agro-climatic conditions of sub-tropical and arid regions of our country. It grows very well in tropical, sub-tropical, sub-mountain and even arid regions. The tree does well in well drained, rich, loam, clayey and even sandy soils.

Terminalia bellirica (Bahera)

Terminalia bellirica (Bahera) tree is structurally very big, has a tall trunk and a large spreading crown. It is one of the more sturdy, durable, pollution resistant and functional trees for city roads and state highways. The tree sheds leaves in April and soon after grows new foliage which is a startling shade of deep crimson. It is also fairly resistant to drought. However, it cannot be used in internal residential streets because its foliage and fruit litters a lot. This tree grows in well drained, deep, sandy as well as clay loam soils. It does best in tropical, sub-tropical, sub-montane and arid regions.

Bischofia javanica (Bisho wood)

Bischofia is a large Indian tree. It has dark green foliage and is evergreen with a beautiful crown. The tree is very neat and does not spread litter. It is durable, hardy, pollution tolerant and extremely good for road side plantation in urban areas. It makes an excellent tree for wide city streets and provides excellent shade and makes very good canopies. It fills up the entire space between buildings and roads with greenery. It is highly suitable for landscaping and beautification of city highways.

This tree grows well in tropical, sub-tropical, sub-mountain and sub-Himalayan tracts. It needs well drained, loam soils with adequate arrangements of irrigation.

Polyalthia longifolia (The Mast tree)

This tree develops tall straight trunks and excellent lateral crowns that make it an ideal tree for growing around narrow city roads. It is very elegant, produces numerous branches that grow horizontally from different parts of the trunk and can provide a green cover on one or two lane roads. The trunk of the tree can be raised to any desirable height.

The tree remains evergreen throughout the year except early summer months when it sheds leaves for a very short time. This tree is slow growing but is extremely hardy, sturdy and durable. It plays a role in purifying the environment and stands extreme environmental pollution - especially toxins from automobiles. It requires minimum care and maintenance.

It grows well in the agro-climatic conditions obtained in tropical, sub-tropical, sub-temperate and sub-mountainous areas upto 3000 feet above sea level. The tree grows well in rich, fertile, neutral and well drained sandy loam and clay loam soils. It does best in bright, sunny spots. Young saplings need abundant and frequent watering.

Cedrela Tuna (Tun)

Tun is one of the most beautiful and functional trees for plantation around city roads. The tree has a large structure and dark green foliage. Tun is partially deciduous and sheds leaves in winter season. This unique characteristic of the tree becoming almost leafless in winter season makes it ideal for planting in parking lots. New foliage appears in early spring. The trunk of the tree can be raised as a single stem up to any desirable height. The tree develops an excellent spreading crown. This tree is very durable, and pollution resistant. It is very neat and does not spread litter. The tree is indigenous to India and grows well in tropical, sub-tropical and even sub-mountain areas. The Tun tree performs well in loam, sandy loam and clay loam soils that have good drainage.

Hardwickia binnata (Anjan)

It is a very ornamental and decorative Indian tree having drooping branches. Anjan is structurally large and is good for creating avenues on city roads. The tree is hardy, durable and does not spread litter. It sheds leaves in early summer months for a short period and soon grows new red tinged foliage.

The tree grows well is tropical, sub-tropical, sub-mountain and arid regions. Neutral sandy and loam, soils rich in organic matter are good for its growth. The Anjan tree also performs well in shallow and gravelly soils that have good drainage.

Madhuca latifolia (Mahua)

Mahua is large sized Indian tree that develops a very strong trunk that stands like a rock. The trunk can be trained to any desirable height. The tree develops an excellent crown. It has dense dark green foliage. The new leaves are bright coppery in colour. The tree is deciduous, sheds leaves in March for a short time. New leaves appear soon. The tree is slow growing but very hardy and durable and has a long life.

All kinds of tropical, sub-tropical and moderately dry type of climate is good for the growth of this plant. It prefers light well drained soil, but grows equally well in rocky, sandy and heavy soils.

Pterospermum acerifolium (Kanak Champa)

Pterospermum acerifolium (Kanak Champa) is a large Indian tree. It has a strong trunk that can be trained to any desired height. It develops wide spreading crown. The tree is durable, hardy and fairly pollution tolerant. Its foliage is dense and evergreen that provides good shade making it very suitable for providing shade on urban roads. Trees bear golden and whitish coloured fragrant flowers in summer months from March to June.

The tree grows well in tropical, sub-tropical, sub-mountain and climate obtained in the sub-Himalayan tracts. Moist loam soils are preferable for ideal growth but it does very well in any kind of well drained soil that may even be slightly alkaline.

Pinus Longifolia (Indian Pine)

Pinus Longifolia (Indian Pine) is a large tree that attains a height of more than 70 ft. It develops a straight tall trunk and massive spreading crown. Pine is deciduous, shedding leaves in early summer months for a short period. New leaves appear soon thereafter. The tree is very attractive and suitable for growing around wide city roads. Although the origin of the tree is the foothills of Himalayas, it has grown wonderfully well in the plains and sub-mountain regions of Northern India at heights of 1500 - 6000 feet above sea level. The tree is slow growing but is hardy, durable and pollution resistant and therefore suitable for growing in urban habitats. The Pine tree grows best in full sunlight. Soil for it need not be rich but should be well drained. Pine grows on rocky slopes and on different kinds of loam, sandy loam, clay loam soils where fertility may be low but drainage is excellent. Pinus Longifolia is drought resistant and once established will not require much care.

10

FLOWERING TREES FOR CITY PUBLIC PARKS, HOMES AND OTHER OPEN SPACES

FLOWERING trees in full bloom are a feast for the eyes. There are over 800 different beautiful varieties of trees across the world. Described in this chapter are a few of these that are suitable to agro-climatic conditions of this region. They are ones that look pretty when they are in bloom and very attractive even when the rest of the year when they are not in bloom.

All of these trees are structurally small or medium in size and do not grow large enough to develop the required kind of tall straight trunks and effective crowns required for city roads. Hence, they are most appropriate for growing in protected places of the city that include public parks, spaces around all public and private buildings as well as homes where they receive extra care.

Flowering trees enhance the urban elements and look exceptional during blooming periods and brighten the city landscape with colour. Planting the flowering trees at close spacing creates an excellent texture of branches and foliage. The branches intermingle and develop a strong network for a dense crown that creates a magnificent floral display when the trees are in bloom. Using one or two species in a planned manner in rows or numerous kinds of formal or informal settings will put up a mass effect of colour.

In parks, around buildings and in homes these flowering trees can be combined with flowering shrubs. While the flowering tree can be trained and raised above the height of shrubs, the colourful shrubs can cover up the entire space around the trunk of the tree, thus putting up an excellent, artistic and floral display all year round. Here is an elaborate description of some flowering trees that are suitable for our agro-climatic conditions.

Cassia nodosa (The Pink Mohur)

Cassia nodosa (Pink Mohur) is undoubtedly the most beautiful of all flowering trees. The tree produces ostentatiously brilliant rose pink flowers in huge clusters. The tree is totally leafless when it starts flowering in early summer months and looks like a huge bouquet of flowers. The flowering period coinciding with the flush of new shoots and leaves continues intermittently up to July-August.

This tree is native of Java, Malaya and Sumatra. Structurally it is a medium sized tree. It has a graceful spreading crown. The tree is leafless in winter and spring season. This tree performs well in tropical, sub-tropical, sub-mountain, temperate and even arid regions. It needs well drained loam soils rich in organic matter.

Cassia spectablis is another kind of Cassia that bears brilliant yellow flowers in winter season.

Lagerstroemia rosea (Queen's flower)

Lagerstroemia rosea (Queen's flower) is an indigenous tree and due to its superior qualities it is rightly named Pride of India too. It is a medium sized tree that is structurally very strong. It is durable and hardy and stands pollution well. This tree partly sheds leaves in winter months and new leaves appear in spring season.

There are many species of this tree. Two of them are very popular. These bear bright pink and purple flowers that bloom profusely from April to August. The tree starts growth in spring continuing into the autumn months of August-September. With each new flush, flowering starts and continues alternately ceasing and starting during this period. In fact, the tree continues to bloom almost throughout the summer season and is strikingly attractive when it is in full bloom. The flowers are produced at the ends of the branches that get loaded with lovely flowers in big sized panicles.

Well drained loam soils rich in organic matter are good for the growth and flowering of this plant. This tree is very hardy and can grow very well in a wide range of climatic and soil conditions. All kinds of climate varying from tropical zone to dry hot as well as extreme cold up to the semi-hill areas with minimum temperatures as low as 25 degrees F are suitable for its growth. It is an excellent tree for growing in parks, open spaces and around public and private buildings. It should be used extensively for beautification and aesthetic plantations in the urban areas.

Jacaranda mimosifolia (Nili Gul Mohur)

Jacaranda mimosifolia (Nili Gul Mohur) is a medium sized tree. It is extensively grown in India for its beauty of tree structure, lovely foliage and massive mauve flowers. It is one of the most beautiful flowering trees. Jacaranda bears brilliant purple blue flowers that appear in big panicles intermittently in spring and summer seasons. It is a deciduous tree that becomes almost leafless in winter months and gets new growth starting in late spring.

The original home of the tree is Brazil but it is growing very well in the variable climatic conditions obtained in India. It is excellent for growing in tropical, sub-tropical, temperate and arid zones. The tree grows well in well-drained loam soils rich in organic matter. It is quite hardy, fast growing and stands pollution of the urban areas.

Cassia fistula (Amaltas)

Cassia fistula (Amaltas) is a beautiful flowering tree. Long, drooping sprays of bright yellow flowers clothe the tree in a mantle of gold in summer months. The flowers are deliciously fragrant. Amaltas provides a splash effect of colour and is a sight to behold when in bloom.

   The tree is very hardy, durable and drought and frost resistant. It can grow in a wide range of climatic conditions ranging from tropical, sub-tropical and arid regions. The plant grows well in properly drained sandy loam, loam and even clay loam soils. It can grow even in poor quality soils. The tree is medium sized. It is excellent for growing around parks and public buildings where this plant adds lot of colour at the time of blooming. The tree sheds leaves in early summer months. Young leaves are coppery-red in colour that appear in summer along with flowers. It is a native of India. Its leaves are inedible to cattle, which makes it suitable for growing in unprotected public places.

Delonix regia (Gul Mohur)

Delonix regia (Gul Mohur) is one of most striking flowering trees. The tree produces a brilliant mass of scarlet flowers in late spring and early summer months. The foliage of tree is attractive. In winter months, tree becomes leafless. Structurally it is a medium sized tree. This tree is most suitable for planting around parks and public buildings. Close planting in rows at spacing of 10 feet will be ideal for obtaining excellent beauty of flowers and foliage. Tree is a native of Madagascar and thrives best in dry hot climate. It can tolerate heat but not frost. Thrives in hot dry climate of tropical, sub-tropical, temperate and sub-mountain regions up to 4000 feet above mean sea level. Loam, well drained soils rich in organic matter are ideal for its growth and good performance.

Bauhinia variegata (Kachnar)

Bauhinia variegata (Kachnar) is a medium sized tree, fairly hardy, durable, and stands urban pollution. It is deciduous, sheds leaves in winter months and becomes bare from November to March. New foliage appears in late spring. This tree blooms profusely, bears pink, purple and white flowers, which appear in clusters in spring season when the tree is leafless. This tree blooms like cherry blossoms and is excellent for plantation in parks, open spaces and public and private buildings.

It is native to India and grows best in tropical, sub-tropical, sub-mountain and even arid zones up to 4000 ft. above sea level. It can grow in well drained loam, clay, sandy loam and rocky soils.

There is another genus of Bauhinia tree called Bauhinia blakeana that bears orchid like flowers rose purple and deep purple in colour during winter season. The flowers are produced in abundance and do not fade for a long time.

Saraca indica (Sita Ashok)

Saraca indica (Sita Ashok) is a medium sized evergreen tree, structurally strong, very hardy and durable. It is fairly resistant to pollution of the urban habitat. It is a beautiful Indian tree and bears large compact clusters of crimson coloured flowers that have a delicate scent in summer season. The foliage of this tree is long, dark green, shining and very attractive. Sita Ashok is considered as a sacred tree dedicated to the God of Love (Kama Deva).

This tree grows well in hot and dry tropical, sub-tropical, semi-cold, climate upto 2000 ft altitude. The tree is slow growing but is excellent for parks, open spaces, public and private buildings and should be used extensively.

The tree needs moist, rich, well-drained loam soils and can tolerate alkaline and saline soils. It can grow at a better pace if it is given good organic and inorganic manures and fertilizers etc. during growing season.

Crataeva religiosa (Barna)

Crataeva religiosa (Barna) is a medium sized tree. The tree is deciduous that sheds leaves in winter months and sprouts new leaves in late spring season. It is hardy and drought resistant. It has an artistic structural frame. Barna is one of the best native trees, bearing whitish flowers that turn creamy to pale yellow in summer months. The tree gets completely covered with flowers and looks spectacular. Since it is indigenous and has good qualities it should be extensively used for plantation in parks, open spaces, around public and private buildings.

This tree grows well in a wide range of climatic conditions ranging from tropical, sub-tropical, sub-mountain and arid regions. It is slow growing, has a deep root system and does well in all kinds of well drained clayey, sandy and loam soils, rich in organic matter.

Acacia auriculiformis (Australian Kikar)

Acacia auriculiformis (Australian Kikar) is medium sized, evergreen, fast growing, very hardy, sturdy durable and drought resistant. The tree starts producing bright yellow flowers profusely in autumn months. The flowering period is more than six months from October to March. Flowering continues into winter season and up to the end of spring season.

This tree is native of Australia but grows very well all over India in a wide range of climatic conditions obtained in tropical, sub-tropical, sub-mountain and arid regions. It puts up excellent growth in all kinds of soils such as loam, clay and sandy loam as well as stony soils but needs good drainage.

Tabebuia rosea

(Basant Rani) Tabebuia rosea (Basant Rani) is a medium sized tree, fairly hardy, sturdy and durable but a little slow growing. It stands environmental pollution of cities. It is a deciduous tree that sheds leaves in winter months.

The tree is strikingly attractive when laden with pink flowers in leafless conditions in spring season. There are two species of this tree - one bears brilliant pink flowers and the other bears brilliant yellow flowers. It is highly suitable for parks, around public and private buildings.

The original home of this tree is Mexico and Brazil but it grows well in the hot, moist climate of tropical, sub-tropical and temperate zones of our country.

Callistemon lanceolatus (Bottle brush)

Callistemon lanceolatus (Bottle brush) is a small graceful tree adorning drooping branches. It is evergreen, very hardy and durable and stands pollution of the urban habitat. This tree is native of Australia but has shown remarkable adaptability in the climatic and soil conditions of India. The tree produces crimson coloured flowers borne on dense cylindrical spikes. The blooming period of this tree is long running from spring into summer and autumn months. Flowering is intermittent during this time when new fresh shoots and leaves appear. Due to its drooping graceful branches, it is an ideal tree for planting around water features. This tree is very suitable for plantation in parks, open spaces, public and private buildings in urban areas.

well drained loam, sandy loam and clay loam soils are good for its growth and performance. There are some more species of Bottle brush that have golden and blue coloured foliage and flowers. These are highly attractive and provide an excellent colour when grown in sunny spots around city parks, open spaces, public and private building.

It does very well in tropical, sub-tropical and even arid regions. All kinds of rich,

Tecomella undulata (Tecoma tree)

Tecomella undulata (Tecoma tree) is a small evergreen tree with drooping branches. It is drought resistant and hardy that thrives best even in dry climate. It is native of the very dry regions of India. This tree should be planted extensively in city parks, open spaces around public and private buildings.

The tree blooms profusely in summer months. The yellowish to deep cadmium orange flowers are strikingly beautiful. When it is in full bloom it produces great beauty in dry parts of India. The tree performs very well in tropical, sub-tropical and arid regions. Well drained loam, sandy loam soils are good for its growth. The tree also tolerates alkalinity.

Tecoma argentea (Tecoma from Argentina)

Tecoma argentea (Tecoma from Argentina) is structurally very small, evergreen, very hardy, durable and drought resistant. It blooms profusely in hot summer months and produces brilliant yellow strikingly beautiful flowers. It is gorgeous when it is in full bloom. The original home of this tree is Argentina but it is growing very well in all kinds of climatic zones i.e. tropical, sub-tropical and arid areas in India.

Due to the hardiness and its beauty of flowers and foliage it should be used extensively as a flowering tree in parks, open spaces, around public and private buildings in urban areas. It is suitable for growing in all kinds of well drained clayey, sandy, silt and loam soils.

Millettia ovalifolia (Moulmein Rose Wood)

Millettia ovalifolia (Moulmein Rose Wood) is structurally a small to medium sized tree. It is fairly hardy and durable and stands pollution of urban areas very well. It is a deciduous tree that sheds leaves in winter. New leaves appear in early summer months. The tree is a glorious sight when it profusely bears massive purple and bright lilac flowers in spring and early summer season. During this time it is intermittently totally leafless. Due to its beautiful structure foliage and flowers, it is one of the good flowering trees suitable for plantation in city parks and other open spaces around public and private buildings. This tree is native of tropical India and Burma and grows well in tropical, sub-tropical, temperate and sub- montane zones.

All kinds of loam, sandy loam, clay loam soils that have drainage are good for its growth and performance.

11

ACHIEVING 100 PERCENT SUCCESS IN GROWING TREES IN URBAN AREAS

TREES not only help create a suitable living environment but also contribute to cleaner air that helps contain pollution in urban areas. The rapid growth in population and exponential development across the country makes tree plantation a low priority. This has to change and tree planting should be seen really as the solution to a lot of urban environmental pollution problems.

Growing trees in urban areas however, is an arduous task One of the major challenges in being successful with planting trees in cities is that as the population is increasing rapidly so are the number of automobiles. Vehicular traffic is very damaging to air quality. Pollution in most of our cities has touched alarming levels. All this environmental pollution causes damage to plants and vegetation. Poisonous gases like carbon-monoxide, hydrocarbons, sulphuric acid, lead as well as dust, fly ash and suspended particulate matter create unhealthy conditions in cities. Poor air quality damages trees and is a growth retardant for trees.

Tree plantation has low success rates when they are planted as saplings. Thousands of saplings are planted every year in cities without much result. A way to manage this is to focus on a results-oriented program. Lay stress on growing trees successfully and not merely on the uncountable saplings planted with nil results. Plantating one street successfully is decisively better than planting ten streets with poor standards. The latter is not just a waste of money but also numerous years without any achievement.

11.1 Photograph of a city in Punjab. It is demonstrative of the treeless skyline that makes for unhealthy, drab living. The scorching heat, dust, glare, polluted air, and unattractive surroundings are a test of peoples physical and mental endurance

There are five simple steps to obtain 100 percent success.

1. Select the right kind of species
2. Raise saplings in a nursery. Grow them to a very large size before transplanting
3. Use very high specifications for plantation and maintenance
4. Provide protection to saplings with strong guards
5. Train the saplings to the desired height so that extensive views of the city are not blocked

Selecting Right Kind Of Species

It is important to select the right kind of trees that should be planted to bring about improvement in the environmental conditions of the urban areas. Just as a man is a unit of society and for creating a better social order in the world, the total thrust is on the development of man's psychologies and culture. Similarly a tree is one of the important units for improving the quality of our physical environment. It is, therefore, essential that trees chosen for urban plantation program have excellent qualities.

Only sturdy, hardy, durable, functional trees that are able to stand stress from environmental pollution should be selected. They should also be attractive, meet aesthetic requirements, be low maintenance and suit agro-climatic conditions. Some outstanding trees that meet these requirements have been described in this book and their important features are highlighted with photographs.

Many planners are attracted by exotic kinds of trees because they are unusual, rare, look more appealing than native trees.

Native trees are considered common and coarse compared to exotic trees. Contrary to this belief, exotic kinds are difficult to grow. They are short lived and are never really healthy no matter how well looked after. As compared to them the indigenous species are lustrous, healthy and thrive with little care. The real point is that when we have a wealth of native trees that are not only functional and attractive there is no need to use foreign kinds. We should adopt local trees and reject the exotic ones.

Raising Large Sized Plants In Nurseries

It is important to give very high priority to the nursery production work. Plants in nurseries should be developed to a large size. Young plants are like children needing extraordinary care for up to the age of 2 to 3 years. Young saplings should not be taken to the field to face extremes of weather conditions such as extreme heat, cold, exposure to hot and cold winds, excessive neglect due to untimely availability of water, food and shelter etc.

Commonly available hi-tech poly house facilities can be used in plant nurseries to raise the required large sized plants in a short period of time. Young saplings in the nursery should be provided adequate space for growth and development. Dense crowding will not let them develop strong structures and root systems. Unless emphasis is laid on developing the right-sized excellent stock in nurseries, no large scale program for plantation can be executed. Plants raised in large sized poly bags and having strong thick stems, well developed root system, nicely trained crowns of strong branches and foliage are the minimum requirement for successful tree plantation.

11.2 Develop plants in nurseries to as big a size as possible. In advanced countries, like the U.S. tree saplings of around 3 to 4 inches caliper thickness of the stem are developed in the nurseries and then taken to the planting site. Photograph shows the large sized plants developed in the nursery in high density polythene bags of 16" x16" size.

Good Specifications For Plantation And Maintenance

Good specifications for plantation and maintenance are also very important. It is necessary that the best possible norms for maintenance including an intensive program of watering, feeding, hoeing, plant protection and even periodical washing of foliage is carried out.

Pits of suitable size should be prepared and filled up with right kind of mixtures consisting of good quality soil, sand, cattle manure, bone-meal and super-phosphate. Phosphate is one of the major nutrients for plants but does not get easily dissolved in water so it does not penetrate into the root zone. Therefore, this fertilizer both in organic and inorganic form should be mixed in the soil so that it continues to become readily available to the growing roots of the plant for a very long period especially during its initial life until the plants gets fully established. These practices exist in practically all advanced countries of the world and must be adopted in India to obtain speedy growth as well as strength of plants.

Providing Sturdy And Functional Tree Guards

A tree guard is an important requirement for obtaining 100% success in implementing effective tree plantation programs around city roads. Young saplings in cities have to survive a lot of physical abuse. Damage to the trunk and bark by stray cattle and even human beings is quite common. It takes about one to two growing seasons to heal the wound caused to the plants. Therefore, tree guards are required. They should be sturdy, functional, economical, easy to remove and reuse and also easy to transport.

11.3 Photograph of a 5-year old tree protected with a tree guard shows good growth. On the other hand, a tree without a tree guard is much smaller.

Training Young Saplings

Training trees grown on the sides of the roads is an essential requirement. Large structured trees can create excellent design if the trunks are raised very high and crowns are developed at the top. It is necessary to modulate the spaces of the city with trees vertically and create ceilings with greater variability in transparency and height. Emphasis should be laid on visibility, maximum sunlight and a continuity of the extensive areas of the city. This is possible only by raising the trunk and crown of the tree as high as possible from the ground.

The obvious advantage of developing roadside trees in this manner is that it enables the visibility of architectural elements and broad views of the vast areas of the city. The entire space around city streets gets complete sunlight. The winter sun is able to penetrate onto roads making them warmer and brighter. In summer months, the crowns of trees provide shade and create an excellent pattern of tree branches and foliage on the road. The street space will broaden and open up and will not cause obstruction to the movement of traffic especially tall buses and trucks etc.

Almost all kinds of trees start branching and developing side branches out of the main stem. Therefore, such undesirable growth has to be removed constantly until the trunks and the crowns are raised and developed upto the desired height.

11.4 The photographs show the trunk of the trees raised as single stem upto a considerable height and then crown is developed.

BIBLIOGRAPHY

Flowering Trees in India by Dr M. S. Randhawa .Published by Indian Council of Agricultural Research, New Delhi. Printed in April 1957 by S.N. Guha Ray at Sree Saraswaty Press Limited, Calcutta -9.

Flowering Trees and Shrubs in India by Cowen D.V. Published by Tacker and Co. in 1950.

Beautifying India by Dr M. S. Randhawa. Rajkamal Publications Ltd. Bombay, Delhi.

Trees of Delhi by Pradip Kumar Published by Dorling Kindersley (India) Pvt. Ltd. in 2006.

New Lives, New Landscapes by Nan Fairbrother, Published by Penguin Books Ltd, Harmondsworth, Middlesex, England. 1972.

Trees in Urban Design by Henry F. Arnold. Published by VAN NOSTRAND REINHOLD COMPANY, NEW YORK.

Le Corbusier: Souvenir of 100th birth Anniversary , 1887-1987 Chandigarh. Published at ARUN & RAJIVE Pvt. Ltd., 10, DSIDC Scheme II. Okhla Industrial Area Phase II, New Delhi -110020.

Gardens of Paradise by John Brookes. Wiedenfeld and Nicolson, London.

Landscape for Living by Garrett Eckbo. An Architectural Record Book with Duell, Sloan, & Pearce.

Techniques of Landscape Architecture by A.E. Weddle,Institute of landscape Architects. Published by HEINEMANN: LONDON

Beautiful Gardens by Dr M. S. Randhawa. Published by Indian Council of Agricultural Research, New Delhi. January 1971.

Exotica International by Dr Alfred Byrd Graf, Volume 1 and 2. Roehrs Company Publishers,

New Jersey, USA.

The Art of Home Landscaping by Garrett Eckbo, Mcgraw Hill Book Company, New York, Toronto, London.

Flowering Trees of the World by Edwin A. Menninger, Published by Hearthside Press Incorporated Publishers, New York.

Celebrating Chandigarh -50 years of the Idea, 9-11 January 1999, Edited by Jaspreet Takhar. Published by Thomson Press, New Delhi.

Gardening in India by S. Percy Lancaster. Published by Mohan Primlani, Oxford & IBH Publishing Co., 66, Janpath, New Delhi.

Urban and Rural Planning Thought prepared and got published by the School of Planning and Architecture, Indraprastha Estate, New Delhi, December 1968.

New Western Garden Book edited by Sunset Books: David E. Clark, Lane Publishing Co., Menlo Park, California.

Flowering Shrubs by B.P. Pal and Krishnamurthi. Published by Indian Council of Agricultural Research, New Delhi. 1967.

100 Beautiful Trees of India by Charles McCann, D.B. Taraporevala Sons & Co Private Ltd., 210, Dr. D. Naoroji Road, Bombay -1.

Landscape Design, Landscape Construction and Superintendence, Landscape Drafting, Landscape semi-Public Grounds and Land sub Division, Landscape Mapping and field work, Landscape salesmanship and office practice, Published by Landscape School DES MOINES LOWA, USA.

Lawn and Gardens by S.L. Jindal, Publication Division, Ministry of Information and Broadcasting, Government of India, October 1982.

Flowering Shrubs in India by S.L. Jindal, Publication Division, Ministry of Information and Broadcasting, Government of India, November 1970.

Home Gardening by P.P. Trivedi, . Published by Indian Council of Agricultural Research, New Delhi. January 1983.

Better Homes and Gardens, Des Moines, Meredith Corporation, New York, 1968.

The Complete Book of Gardening edited by Michael Wright. Published by Ebury Press and Michael Joseph.

Flowers of the World by Frances Perry. Publisher: HAMLYN, London, New York, Sydney Toronto.

How to Grow and Use Annuals, Basic Gardening, Garden Colour -Annuals and Perennials, Gardening in Containers, Published by Sunset Books and Sunset Magazine. Lane Publishing Co., Menlo Park, California.

Complete Library of the Garden, Vol I, II, & III. Published by the Readers Digest Association.

Plants of the Punjab by C.J.Bamber. Published by M/s Bishan Singh, Mahendra Pal Singh, 23 A, New Connaught Place, Dehra Dun and M/s Periodical Experts, D-42, Vivek Vihar, Delhi -110030, 1976.

A Forest Flora for the Punjab by R.N. Parker. Published by M/s Bishan Singh, Mahendra Pal Singh, 23 A, New Connaught Place, Dehra Dun and M/s Periodical Experts, D-42, Vivek Vihar, Delhi -110030, 1973.

The mango - A Hand Book. Published by Indian Council of Agricultural Research, New Delhi. January 1983.

Fruit Culture in India by Sham Singh & Dr. S. Krishnamurthy & S.L. Katyal. Published by Indian Council of Agricultural Research, New Delhi.

Fruit Growing in India by W.B.Hayes. Published by Kitabistan, Allahbab.

Beautiful Climbers of India by B.P.Pal. Published by Indian Council of Agricultural Research, New Delhi.

The Lawn Expert by Dr. D.G. Hessayon. Published by Britannica House, England.

The House Plant Expert by Dr. D.G. Hessayon. Published by Britannica House, England.

Turf Management for Golf Courses by James B. Bread. Published by John Wiley & Sons, INC, United States, Printed in Canada.

The Rose in India by B.P.Pal. Published by Indian Council of Agricultural Research, New Delhi.

Pruning and Training of Fruit Trees by Cooperative Extension Service, IOWA State University of Science and Technology, AMES, IOWA.

Modern Architecture by Vincent Scully, Jr. Allied Publishers Private Limited, Bombay, New Delhi, Calcutta, Madras, Bangalore.

Pochas Garden Guide by Bhanu L. Desai. Published by Pestonjee P. Posha & Sons, Poona-1.

Lawns and Gardens by S.L.Jindal. Published by Ministry of Information and Broadcasting, Government of India.

Climatological Features of Chandigarh by Y.Agnihotri, R.C.Bansal, Prahlad Singh, S.P.Mittal. Published by Central Soil & Water Conservation Research and Training Institute, Chandigarh.

All About House Plants by William Davidson. Published by Spring Books, London, New York, Sydney, Toronto.

Indoor Garden Book by John Brookes, Published by Dorling Kindersley, London.

Gardens Through the Ages by Dr. Mohinder Singh Randhawa. Published by The MAC MILLAN Company of India Limited, Delhi, Bombay, Calcutta, Madras.

IKEBANA - The Art of Japanese Flower Arrangement by Georgie Davidson and Beata Bishop. Published by W.H. ALLEN, London, 1967.

Planning a Landscape Garden by L.N.Birla. Published by The Royal Agri- Horticultural Society of India, 1, Alipur Road, Calcutta.

Horticultural Operations the Year Round by Buta Singh Sekhon. Published by Punjab Agricultural University, Ludhiana.

CHRYSANTHEMUMS by Brandford Bearce and Others. Published by The New York State Extension Service Chrysanthemum School with cooperation of New York State Flower Growers Association, June 1964.

Bougainvilleas by B.P.Pal and Vishnu Swarup. Published by Indian Council of Agricultural Research, New Delhi.

Ornamental Horticulture in India by G.S.Randhawa. Published by Today & Tomorrow's Printers & Publishers, New Delhi.

Cacti and other Succulents by Katie Meadow. Published by Broombacher Books, Richmond, California.

Foliage House Plants by James Underwood Crockett. Published by Time- Life Books, Alexandria, Virgenia.

The Dictionary of House Garden Plants by Roy Hay and Patrick M. Synge. Published by Ebury Press and Michael Joseph, Great Britain.

Planning and Planting Design of Home Garden by Bhanul L. Desai. Published by Indian Council of Agricultural Research, New Delhi.

House Plants by Margaret E. Jones. Published by Penguin Books, Great Britain, 1962.

Water Plants by E.B. Singh Bhadri & B.L. Desai. Published by Indian Council of Agricultural Research, New Delhi.

Tropical Plants by Dorothy and Bob Hargreaves. Published by Hargreaves Company. INC, Kailua, Hawaii, USA.

Cultivation of Bulbous Plants in India by K.S.Gopalaswamiengar. Published by Mysore Horticultural Society.

ABC of Chrysanthemums by W.E. Shewell Cooper. Published by The English Universities Press Ltd. 102, New Gate Street, London.

Hawaii Blossoms by Dorathy and Bob Hargreaves. Published by Hargeaves Company. INC, Kailua, Hawaii.

Dahlia Growing by Swami Vinayananda. Published by Associated Publishing Company, New Delhi.

Rose Growing in the Tropics by B.S.Bhatcharji. Published by Thacker Spink & Co.Private Ltd. Calcutta.

Creating a Herb Garden by Anthony Gardiner. Published by Chartwell Books INC. New Jersey, 1995.

Home Growing by Ann Bonar & Others. Published by Marshall Cavendish Books Limited, 58, Old Compton Street, London.

Index

Made in the USA
Middletown, DE
16 October 2022

12875516R00119